THE PHONE RANG

THE ESSENTIAL PLAYBOOK FOR BUSINESS SUCCESS

BOB MARSHALL

JK FRANKS MEDIA, LLC

Copyright © 2024 by Bob Marshall

All rights reserved.

No part of this book may be reproduced in any form or by any electronic or mechanical means, including information storage and retrieval systems, without written permission from the author, except for the use of brief quotations in a book review.

Copyright © 2024 by Bob Marshall
eBook. 978-1-964509-91-4
Paperback 978-1-964509-92-1
Hardback 979-8-9884788-1-2

Published by JKF Media LLC, 2024
Editor: Debra Riggle

Email the author at bob@themarshallplan.org
Friend him on Facebook at facebook.com/BobMarshallsERM
Visit the author's website at themarshallplan.org OR enroll in Bob's masterclass at elite.recruitmasterclass.com/bigbiller

First Edition

I have been saved many times in my life. You don't make it far in life without a little help. Whether it be genes or skill or just plain dumb luck.

For

Linda, Ed, Alan, Chuck, Ron, David & Kevin...

You know who you are!

"Success is the sum of small efforts, repeated day in and day out."

- ROBERT COLLIER

PREFACE

Yes, my roots are firmly planted in the world of recruiting. It's a field that demands a deep understanding of people – what drives them, motivates them, and helps them excel. But as I've coached and consulted with businesses across diverse industries, I've come to realize that the principles driving success are strikingly universal. Whether you're in sales, technology, healthcare, or running your own entrepreneurial venture, the same core elements are at play.

At the heart of any successful business lies exceptional talent. Identifying that talent, nurturing it, and providing the right environment for it to flourish is the key to building high-performing teams. It's about implementing systems, training, and support mechanisms that allow people to reach their full potential. Whether it's finding the right candidate for a crucial role or developing your sales team into a powerhouse, these fundamentals remain the same.

Recruiting also offers a unique lens through which to study deal-making, client relationships, and navigating complex landscapes. Understanding motivations, overcoming objections, and cultivating trust are skills that will propel you forward in any business. The strategies I've honed in the dynamic recruiting world are designed to empower you to do just that.

So, while the stories in this book may often draw from my expertise in recruiting, consider this your invitation to apply these lessons to your specific field. Think of it as a roadmap to building a winning team, delivering exceptional value to your clients, and achieving your ambitious business goals – whatever they may be.

FOREWORD

Paul Hawkinson, Editor, "The Fordyce Letter"

"Bob Marshall is one of those guys whose masterful grasp of the recruiting and search business comes from working the daily grind in the trenches. Entering this business as an Account Executive for a Management Recruiters office in 1980, he quickly became a billing superstar, winning national awards and recognition for his production. MR was so impressed with him that he was made Western Regional Manager over 60 offices where he became MR's top trainer.

In 1986 he went into business for himself where he developed **The Marshall Plan**, a well-known and highly regarded methodology for becoming an above average search and recruiting practitioner. Bob has written occasionally for *The Fordyce Letter* as well as other publications in the industry and his contributions demonstrate his insights into the process that are often overlooked by others. Bob's training program emphasizes the formula approach to success and his comparisons to the manufacturing business put an interesting twist to the writings in his new training manual."

"This is no-nonsense information that should be in everyone's training regimen – **a definite two thumbs up**."

David Alexander - Adecco, Soliant

"Bob Marshall is a speaker's speaker and a trainer's trainer. He has a gift for taking the cornerstones of the business and compelling people and teams to not only hone their skills but to execute. We've had Bob engage our teams a number of times over the last few years and our groups always come away more focused on the core and more energized to perform. Come ready to learn because this man knows the business and will make you better!"

CONTENTS

PART 1
THE FOUNDATION

1. INTRODUCTION	3
2. BUSINESS IS WAR	6
3. WHAT WE ARE	11
4. SECURING LOYALTY	16

PART 2
BECOMING EXCELLENT

5. BECOMING A BIG BILLER	23
6. FIND YOUR PASSION	26
7. MARKETING CALLS	30
8. PAINKILLERS	39
9. QUALIFYING THE JOB ORDER	42
10. YOUR MANUFACTURING PLANT	49
11. SMALL CAN BE BIG	52

PART 3
GROWTH STRATEGIES

12. THE 12 PRINCIPLES	57
13. THE PERFECT RECRUITER	59
14. NAVIGATING INDUSTRY CYCLES	64
15. AHOY, MATE! CHANGES AHEAD	66
16. BUILDING YOUR PRACTICE	70
17. ALIGNMENT WITH YOUR GOALS	73
18. MARKETING 101	76
19. HOW TO ACQUIRE THE RIGHT ATTITUDE	80
20. CLIMBING THE MOUNTAIN	88
21. CONVERSATION WITH A SUPERSTAR	95
Wisdom of 'Robocruiter' and the Total Account Executive, Part One	95

22. CLOSING AND CLOSES	102
23. THE POWER OF GOAL SETTING	113
24. CULTIVATING A GROWTH MINDSET	116

PART 4
PROFESSIONAL ADVANCEMENT

25. OBJECTION RESPONSES	123
26. CREATING A MAGNETIC BRAND	133
27. CONVERSATION WITH A SUPERSTAR	137
Wisdom from 'Robocruiter' and the Total Account Executive, Part Two	137
28. RECRUITING THE CANDIDATE	145
29. MPCS	152
30. BRANCHING OUT	155
31. YOUR BEST INVESTMENT	159
32. BE BAD TO BE GOOD	162

PART 5
MASTERY & INNOVATION

33. PLANNING & ORGANIZATION	167
34. BLUE OCEAN THINKING	175
35. THE SUCCESS PYRAMID	178
36. FOCUS	186
37. YOUR IDEAL CLIENT	190
38. BECOME INVALUABLE	192
39. BE A MASTER CLOSER	197
40. MESSAGES THAT GET RESULTS	200

PART 6
SCALING YOUR BUSINESS

41. GET PAID	207
42. YOUR BUSINESS, YOUR STORY	211
43. MARKETING WATERFALLS	214
44. BEST YEAR EVER	217
45. DEAD HORSES	220
46. MAKE IT SCALABLE	225

47. ATTAINING MASTERY	228
48. LIES THAT DOOM US	231

PART 7
THE FUTURE

49. MOTIVATION	237
50. THE DIRECT TECHNIQUE	239
The Big Biller (BB) Direct Recruiting Technique	239
51. SIGNALS AND NOISE	242
52. A PROVEN METHOD	246
53. WHAT COMES NEXT	248
About the Author	253

Part 1 | The Foundation

"Mastery is not a function of genius, but a function of time invested and persistence applied."
- ANGELA DUCKWORTH

1 INTRODUCTION

ARE YOU READY TO DISCOVER THE SECRETS THAT TOOK ONE ambitious recruiter from average to $1 million in billings within a single year? Meet David, a recruitment professional who reached out to me with a burning question: "Can you teach me how to bill $1 million in the next 12 months?"

I knew I had to choose my next student wisely. Over the years, I've learned to look for a few key traits: raw intelligence, creativity, corporate maturity, tenacity, and work-life balance. David checked all the boxes, and I could see his fixable gaps just waiting to be bridged. And so, our journey began.

The first things I taught David were the three factors that separate recruitment superstars from the rest of the pack. First, they maintain an activity level 2-3 times higher than average, even during market downturns. Second, they relentlessly hone their craft, like Larry Bird practicing free throws between championship games. And third, they operate with an unshakable belief in their own success.

Next, we defined David's battlefield using the 'Law of 1500' and '4% Rule.' By targeting 1500 small-to-midsize companies per quarter and converting 4% into Placements, historical data shows 60 deals can be achieved annually. At a $20,000 average fee, that's the $1 million mark. While huge corporations seem alluring, I cautioned David about their lack of urgency, stifling bureaucracy, and sporadic hiring freezes that can derail a recruiter's momentum.

I impressed upon David, that marketing truly is King in this business. By making marketing calls every single day, he would uncover fresh opportunities, sharpen his presentation skills, gather critical market intelligence, and most importantly, remain top-of-mind with hiring managers. In an ever-shifting landscape, this consistent presence allows recruiters to spot emerging trends and adapt quickly.

Perhaps the most challenging lesson for David to implement was engaging in every phase of the recruitment lifecycle on a daily basis. From marketing and recruiting to prepping candidates, checking references, and closing deals, neglecting any one activity leads to skill erosion and wild swings in production. Overcoming the natural aversion to planning, especially the night before, became a transformative habit in keeping David on track.

As David's portfolio of job orders grew, I taught him the art of ruthless qualification. Not every order deserves full effort, and elite recruiters develop a sixth sense for spotting the true gems. Qualifying for urgency and thoroughly capturing specs, while gracefully declining mediocre orders, shifted David's mindset from reactive justification to proactive control.

With each passing week, I watched David's numbers climb as he implemented these proven practices. Setbacks were met with doubled efforts rather than self-doubt. Relationships deepened into genuine partnerships. And as the months flew by, David's unrelenting march toward the $1 million mark became a matter of when, not if.

Twelve months after that fateful phone call, David's final tally stood at $1,010,349.50. A truly remarkable achievement, but not a surprising one. For recruitment success ultimately comes down to faithfully executing on the fundamentals, no matter how simple they may seem. Armed with the right mindset, an extraordinary work ethic, and a sincere commitment to solving clients' problems, any recruiter can replicate David's accomplishment.

My challenge to you, dear reader, is simply this: Decide that you will do what it takes. Stay coachable, never stop learning and growing, and make building real relationships your guiding light. With unwavering dedication, your own $1 million year is closer than you think. And I will show you how!

2 BUSINESS IS WAR

As I pondered the document's description of a recruiter's responsibilities, my mind wandered to the countless other professions out there. Whether you're a salesperson, a consultant, or an entrepreneur, the path to success often follows a similar trajectory.

I thought back to my early days in recruiting when I was just starting to find my footing. I remember setting ambitious goals for myself, visualizing the day when I would finally make it big. But I quickly learned that success wasn't just about dreaming big—it was about putting in the work, day in and day out.

I recall a conversation I had with a fellow recruiter coach named Jerry. We were both attending a conference, and during a break, we got to talking about what it takes to stand out in our field.

"You know, it's not just about making the calls and filling the orders," Jerry said. "It's about going above and beyond. It's about building relationships with your clients, anticipating their needs before they even know they have them."

I nodded in agreement, thinking about the countless hours I had spent researching companies, crafting personalized pitches, and following up with candidates. It was the little things that made all the difference.

But as Jerry and I continued to talk, we realized that the same principles applied to any business. Whether you're selling products or services, the key to success lies in the fundamentals: setting clear goals, developing a plan of action, and executing on that plan with unwavering discipline.

Of course, that's easier said than done. In any competitive field, there are always going to be obstacles and setbacks. But the most successful people are the ones who refuse to let those challenges hold them back. They're the ones who keep pushing forward, even when the odds seem stacked against them.

As I reflected on the lessons I had learned throughout my career, I couldn't help but think of the wisdom imparted by some of the greats. Zig Ziglar once said, "You can have everything in life you want, if you will just help other people get what they want." That simple idea had been a guiding principle for me from the very beginning.

I remember early on in my career, I listened to a seminar led by Og Mandino. He spoke about the importance of setting clear goals and developing a plan to achieve them. "The greatest secret in the world," he said, "is that you can have anything you want if you are willing to give up the belief that you can't have it."

Positive thinking was the buzz word back then, and it still holds true. Those words stuck with me, and I began to apply them to my own life. I started by setting specific, measurable goals for myself. Whether it was hitting a certain number of calls per day or closing a certain number of deals per month, I made sure that I had a clear target to aim for.

But setting goals was just the first step. I also needed to develop a plan of action to achieve them. That meant breaking down my goals into smaller, more manageable tasks and then tackling those tasks one by one.

Of course, even with a solid plan in place, there were still challenges to overcome. Rejection was a constant companion in the world of recruiting, and it was easy to get discouraged when things didn't go my way. But I learned to reframe those setbacks as opportunities for growth.

Keep in mind that failures and setbacks are going to happen. Failure is an event, not a person. We must refuse to let our failures define us, and instead use them as fuel to keep pushing forward.

Looking back on my journey, I realized that success wasn't just about hitting a certain number or reaching a certain milestone. It was about the person I had become along the way. The discipline, the resilience, the unwavering commitment to my goals—those were the things that truly mattered.

What Is It We as Recruiters Do?

Some years ago, I came across a very detailed description of what we, as recruiters, do for a living. This is the first paragraph of that six-page, 1,469-word long document*:

"The basic function of this position is to promote sales of Placement services to customers and prospective customers within the assigned desk specialty. To maintain and develop satisfied customers for the company through proper handling of customers and candidates and cooperate with management in resolving problems in areas of collections, guarantees, and any other negotiations or functions that may be assigned."

It went on to list our nine major responsibilities:

1. Selling Placement Services
2. Account Development
3. Pricing
4. Customer Service
5. Sales Estimates
6. Candidate Development
7. Records and Reports
8. Expense Control
9. Maintain Professional Standards

Does this sound like what you do? While in some ways I admire the detail (and I hope I handle all of those responsibilities effectively on my desk on a daily basis), I am not sure that it gives a true sense of what we recruiters truly do for a living.

To borrow liberally from a recent article of mine, there are five major tasks that we perform on a daily basis—and they all have to do with picking up the telephone!

And yes, in this case, the phone is both representative and practical. For most of us, the phone is the one instrument we can count on to create business opportunities. If your business is more in person or via web-meetings, then substitute that visual metaphor. What it means is the practice of actively connecting with your clients or product line (candidates, in our case). Leaving a voicemail is not active. Sending an email is not active. Crafting a clever newsletter is not active. Those are (at best) supportive or passive marketing activities.

Oh, yes, I hear you. "But Bob, I make money from those emails," or "I've made Placements using voicemails. My client will not pick up the phone or take a meeting."

The response I would give my students is to "Find a new client. One that will respect you as a professional." And yes, you may make money from using more passive techniques, but is it scalable; can you do it consistently and predictably? I would argue the answer to that will generally be no.

3 WHAT WE ARE

First, and foremost...

1. We are **Marketers**. We make daily marketing, or sales, calls. It is our first key to success. In the immortal words of the famous Sidney Boyden who founded Boyden Associates in 1946 (as quoted in "The Headhunters" by John A. Byrne), "When I employed an associate I was interested in a man who could be a business getter and a merchandiser. I was looking for widely acquainted top sales executives. Because the ability to go out and promote business and get business is more important than finding the men. I was least interested in somebody who would know how to track down a man and find him."

2. We are **Recruiters**. We recruit for a living. That means we find prospective recruits who are happy, well-appreciated, making good money, currently working, and we entice them to move for better opportunities (i.e., our search assignment-quality JOs). We don't work with job-hoppers, job-shoppers, or rejects.

3. We are **Discriminators** (in the positive sense of that word). We are especially selective of our job orders, only choosing the best

search assignment quality job orders on which to spend our straight-commission time. These JOs fall into the following three distinct categories:

- Those JOs that have a tremendous urgency attached to filling the position. We are often paid to circumvent the time factor.
- Those JOs that are very difficult positions to fill. This is where our client companies have run ads, offered referral bonuses to their employees, checked with competitors, consulted with colleagues, and extensively interviewed with no success. In these scenarios, the recruiter offers the company a window of opportunity—a 'court of last resort,' if you will.
- Those JOs from forward-thinking client companies who wish to be kept apprised of top-notch talent as those talented people surface, regardless of whether there is an opening.

4. We are **Negotiators**. We pre-prep, prep, educate, debrief, act as buffers, and close our deals.

5. And ultimately, we are **GREAT Salespeople**. We thrive in a marketplace where our normal Marketing Attempt to Marketing Presentation ratio is somewhere between 10% - 25%. We are successful in that marketplace where we only place with 4% of our client base. And we deal, on a daily basis, with emotional people on both sides of our transactions (refrigerator salespeople don't have to worry about their refrigerators changing their minds, getting pregnant, or moving to Topeka)! And we do all of this via the telephone, which effectively eliminates $3/5^{ths}$ of our sales tools. We can only talk and listen. We can't reach out and touch, use body language and physical mirroring, or make eye contact. We must be exceptional to accomplish all that we accomplish!

The Qualities We Possess

Now, what qualities must we possess? I believe that five are essential. We must bring these to the table. They cannot be taught:

1. Intelligence—not Mensa membership, but we must be smart.

2. Creativity—because each phone call, no matter how it starts, may go in a different direction; we must be flexible enough, creative enough, to flow with the call. We must be noted for our flexibility.

3. Corporate Maturity—this is not a function of age, but of maturity at the corporate level. Having the ability to call the CEO of a client company and not being intimidated if we're asked to make that call.

4. Tenacity—this is important in any endeavor. If you want to put a 'star' by one of the most important traits, star this one! The ability 'to hang in there' is critical. This is important in any profession, but especially in ours.

5. Balanced 'X' Factors—any changes in your life—even good ones—produce stress. Stress is a physical, mental, or emotional factor that causes bodily or mental tension. This tension itself is stressful, often leading to illness or depression. So, we must have this element under control.

After these 'Have to Possess...' traits, I like to see the following, but I can live without them:

6. Successful Failures—people who were successful, but their past employers failed them.

7. Positive Hostility—the ability to be confrontive, but in a positive way. We don't want to be a 'professional visitor' where everyone loves us, but nobody buys from us—but we don't want to be purely hostile either, since rapport building is so important to our success.

8. Good Sense of Humor—the ability to not take ourselves too seriously; to be self-effacing. Humor can go a long way in getting us back on the phone. Our job is supposed to be fun. If we carry that humor out with us to our marketplace, it will come back to us.

9. Empathy—the ability to understand both sides, from their points of view.

10. Ego Driven—we must have a big ego. It's amazing to me how a group of Big Billers all fit in the same room at the same time with their giant-sized egos.

11. Need to convince others to do what we want them to do—the ability to want to convince others of the right way to do our business, not to buy off on the first objection when we hear it.

12. Ability to Listen and Give Positive Feedback—this is key; we are not in a profession made up of 'silver-tongued' devils; listen between the lines, don't answer questions too fast; the other side will give us the information we need as long as we listen and give positive feedback.

13. A decisive person—we can't be 'wishy-washy' in our profession.

14. Intuitive—usually our first sense about something, whether it relates to our candidate or to our client company, is true. Go with our intuition. Things don't go sour unless they smell a little along the way.

15. A tight need for Organization and Planning—it's not that we love it, but over time, we become expert at it.

16. A Leader—someone who wants to lead, even if it is just on our own desk—our own manufacturing plant. This trait encompasses many of the preceding ones.

And finally, after all of these, I think of the attributes that the legendary recruitment trainer, **Lou Scott,** spoke about. He used to say that the biggest billers:

1. Ignore conventional wisdom; they are never satisfied with the norm; they play outside the box.

2. Have written goals for measurement; if they are not written down, they are wishes, not goals.

3. Visualize completion of their goals; have a clear visual picture of their goals.

4. Learn to deal with their anxieties regarding their performance; everyone has anxieties; big billing is not the absence of anxiety, but the controlling of anxiety. Courage is not the absence of fear, but positively dealing with that fear. You need fear in order to have courage.

5. Avoid comfort zones; take calculated risks.

6. And, live in the present. Be where you are. When you are at work, be there. When you are at home, be there. But don't be at home when you are at work and don't be at work when you are at home.

4 SECURING LOYALTY

I GET STORIES ALL THE TIME FROM RECRUITERS COMPLAINING about candidates who ghosted the interview or hiring managers who won't return their calls. Securing loyalty mainly depends on three things: working with the right people, having a solid set of ground rules that everyone agrees to, and keeping the process on track.

The Power of Urgency in Recruitment

In the world of recruitment, urgency is the name of the game. Just as in brick-and-mortar retail, where location is everything, in our business, the three most important factors for success are urgency, urgency, and urgency. Now, you might be wondering, where does this urgency come from? Well, let me tell you—it comes from small and mid-size companies. These are the businesses that are driving job creation, accounting for a whopping 65 - 75% of new jobs. So, if you want to succeed as a recruiter, that's where you need to focus your efforts.

The Three Types of Companies That Need Us

As recruiters, we work best with three types of companies:

1. Companies with a tremendous urgency to fill a position.
2. Companies with a difficult position to fill, who have exhausted all other options.
3. Progressive companies that want to stay informed about top talent in their industry.

Our job is to educate these companies on how we work and the value we bring to the table. Remember, education takes place on every call. Either you educate the hiring manager first, or they educate you. The fastest person wins this race. Either you will educate the hiring manager on how you work, first, or they will educate you on how they work, first. And the fastest person wins this race.

The TBMG Job Order Qualifying Technique

To make the most of your time and effort, you need to focus on search assignment quality job orders. That means qualifying each and every job order you write at the front-end, using the TBMG Qualifier Job Order technique.

This six-part methodology helps you determine the quality of your Job Order.

The initial key points to cover are:

1. Contact Information
2. Duties & Responsibilities of the position
3. Salary & Fee
4. The Hiring Process
5. The Recruitment Target information
6. The Personality of the Hiring Manager

You now have the six critical pieces of information—your skeleton JO. Leave it alone at this point. Later call the HM back to get more information. If they are reachable, that is your first positive sign that this is a top quality JO. If not, it is your first sign that this JO is not workable on your terms. What we refer to as a Can't Help JO.

The Theory of Threes

Once you have a qualified job order, it's time to put the Theory of Threes into action. This involves using the power of competition and the fear of loss to create urgency and drive the hiring process forward quickly. At the same time, you need to establish a mutual exchange of cooperation with the hiring manager. This means setting clear expectations and timelines and holding each other accountable for meeting them.

Becoming A Recruiting Doctor

Remember, as a recruiter, you are the expert—just like a doctor. You need to be committed to excellence in your business and establish the procedure for your clients to follow. Don't let hiring managers dictate how you do your job. Educate your clients, maintain open and honest communication, and always strive to be respected first. If you do that, the rest will follow. So, there you have it—the key to success in recruitment on the employer side is urgency, qualifying job orders, and establishing yourself as the expert.

Mastering Candidate Management

Alright, folks, let's talk about the other side of the recruiting coin—candidate management. Because let's face it, without a strong stable of candidates, all the urgency and qualified job orders in the world won't matter.

Building Your Candidate Pipeline

The first step in effective candidate management is building a robust pipeline. This means constantly sourcing, networking, and marketing yourself to top talent in your industry. You want to become the go-to recruiter for the best and brightest. And how do you do that? By leveraging every tool and platform at your disposal. From AI,

LinkedIn, and industry-specific job boards to referrals and good old-fashioned cold calling, you need to be proactive in your approach.

Qualifying and Assessing Candidates

Once you have a pool of potential candidates, it's time to start qualifying and assessing them. This involves more than just looking at resumes—you need to dig deeper to understand their skills, experience, motivations, and career goals.

Conduct thorough interviews, use assessment tools, and most importantly, listen to your candidates. The more you understand them, the better equipped you'll be to match them with the right opportunities. What will be motivating their move to a new job? What might prevent them from moving forward? We will touch more on this in later chapters, but it's important to know more than what a single piece of paper will tell you.

Setting Expectations and Communicating Effectively

Clear communication is the foundation of any successful relationship, and that's especially true when it comes to working with candidates. From the very first interaction, you need to set clear expectations about your process, timeline, and what they can expect from you. Keep your candidates informed at every stage of the process, whether it's giving them feedback after an interview or updating them on the status of a job opportunity. Remember, even if they don't get the job, a positive candidate experience can lead to referrals and future Placements.

This is an area in which I have a firm rule—Pick up the phone. Talk to them live. Text messages, IMs, Voicemails, and Facebook messages are insufficient. Hear their voice. Make them commit to being prepped and ready for the interview. Build that trust and friendship in the most direct means possible.

Preparing Candidates for Interviews and Offers

Your job as a recruiter doesn't end when you submit a candidate for a job. You need to be there every step of the way, from preparing them for interviews to guiding them through the offer process.

Help your candidates understand the company culture, the hiring manager's expectations, and the key points they should emphasize in their interviews. And when an offer comes in, be there to advise them on negotiation strategies and help them make an informed decision.

Building Long-Term Relationships

Finally, remember that candidate management is about more than just filling job orders. It's about building long-term relationships with top talent in your industry. Stay in touch with your placed candidates, offer them career advice and support, and celebrate their successes. By doing so, you'll create a network of loyal candidates who will not only work with you again in the future but will also refer their colleagues and friends.

Conclusion: Putting It All Together

Effective candidate management is just as important as working with urgency and qualifying job orders. By building a strong pipeline, qualifying and assessing candidates, communicating effectively, preparing them for success, and nurturing long-term relationships, you'll set yourself apart as a top recruiter in your industry.

Remember, your candidates are one of your most valuable assets. Treat them with respect, honesty, and professionalism, and they'll become your biggest advocates and the key to your long-term success.

Part 2 | Becoming Excellent

"Continuous improvement is better than delayed perfection."

- MARK TWAIN

5 BECOMING A BIG BILLER

I've seen it time and time again—recruiters who struggle to make ends meet, never quite reaching their full potential. But I've also seen the other side of the coin—the recruiters who consistently bill over a million dollars a year. So, what's the secret? What separates the superstars from the rest of the pack?

Truthfully, it isn't one thing—it's everything. You see, successful recruiting isn't about reinventing the wheel or chasing after the latest trends. It's about finding what works for you and doing more of it. It's about mastering the fundamentals and executing them with precision and consistency. Ultimately, it all comes down to repetitive flawless execution.

Take David, for example. When he first came to me, he was struggling to break six figures. But after a year of working together, he billed over a million dollars. How did he do it? By focusing on the three key factors that separate the superstars: high activity level, continuous skill honing, and attitude—an unshakable belief in his own success.

We started by defining his target market using the 'Law of 1500' and the '4% Rule.' This helped him focus his efforts on the clients and candidates who were most likely to lead to Placements. From there, we emphasized the importance of consistent marketing. David made it a point to reach out to his network every single day, whether it was through phone calls, emails, or social media.

But marketing alone wasn't enough. David also engaged in the full recruitment lifecycle daily, from sourcing and qualifying candidates to closing deals and managing relationships. He qualified his job orders ruthlessly, ensuring that he was only working on opportunities that had a high probability of success.

As David implemented these proven practices, his numbers began to climb. He went from struggling to make a Placement to consistently billing over $80,000 a month. And after a year of faithful execution of the fundamentals, he achieved the milestone of $1,010,349.50 in billings.

But what was the real secret to David's success? He never stopped marketing. Even when he was brimming with job orders and candidates, he continued to reach out to his network and build relationships. He understood that in the world of recruiting, the pipeline is everything. The moment you stop marketing is the moment your business starts to decline.

I've always believed that success in recruiting (and in life) starts with your mindset. It's not about the external circumstances or the challenges you face—it's about how you choose to respond to them. And that's why I'm such a big believer in setting measurable and specific goals.

When I first started working with David, one of the first things we did was sit down and define his goals. We didn't just talk about vague aspirations like 'making more money' or 'being successful.' We got specific. We looked at his current billings, his average Placement fee, and his conversion ratios. From there, we reverse-engineered exactly what he needed to do to hit his target of $1 million in billings.

We broke it down into daily, weekly, monthly and quarterly metrics. How many phone calls did he need to make each day? How many job orders did he need to qualify each week? How many Placements did he need to make each month? By focusing on these details and tracking his progress, David was able to stay on track and make adjustments as needed.

But setting goals was just the beginning. To truly succeed in recruiting, you need to be committed to relentless improvement. The industry is always changing, and what worked yesterday may not work tomorrow. That's why David made it a point to stay on top of the latest trends and technologies.

He attended conferences and workshops, read industry publications, and sought out mentors who could share their wisdom and experience. Together, we experimented frequently with new tools and techniques, from AI-powered candidate sourcing to video interviewing platforms. And as industry leaders, we aren't afraid to try new things, even if they don't always work out.

Through it all, we relied on proven principles that have stood the test of time. The importance of building relationships, the power of persistence, the value of integrity—these are the things that will never go out of style. And by combining these timeless truths with the latest tools and strategies, David was able to achieve remarkable results.

Of course, none of this would have been possible without ongoing mentoring and support. As a recruiter, it's easy to feel like you're on an island, especially when you're first starting out. But having someone to turn to for guidance, encouragement, and accountability can make all the difference.

6 FIND YOUR PASSION

In the world of business, it's easy to get caught up in the features and benefits of our products or services. We're eager to showcase what we have to offer, hoping to dazzle potential clients with our expertise and capabilities. However, we often forget that customers don't care about what we're selling until they know that we genuinely care about them and their needs.

Showing that you care is the foundation of any successful client relationship. It's not just about delivering a high-quality service or product; it's about demonstrating empathy, anticipating their needs, and being authentic in your interactions.

One way to show that you care is by actively listening to your clients. Take the time to understand their challenges, goals, and aspirations. Ask thoughtful questions and pay attention to their responses. By doing so, you'll gain valuable insights into their unique situation and be better equipped to tailor your offerings to meet their specific needs.

Another crucial aspect of showing that you care is anticipating potential issues or delays. No one likes unpleasant surprises, especially when it comes to business. By proactively communicating any potential roadblocks or setbacks, you demonstrate that you're invested in the success of the project and value transparency. This level of honesty and foresight builds trust and strengthens the client relationship.

Empathy is also a powerful tool in showing that you care. Put yourself in your client's shoes and try to understand their perspective. Acknowledge their concerns and validate their feelings. By doing so, you create a deeper connection and show that you're not just interested in making a sale, but in truly understanding and supporting them.

Finally, it's essential to deliver your services with authenticity. Clients can quickly sense when someone is being insincere or disingenuous. Be genuine in your interactions, follow through on your promises, and go above and beyond to exceed their expectations. When you deliver your services with authenticity, you build a reputation for reliability and integrity, which is invaluable in the business world.

Remember that customers don't care about what you offer until they know that you care about them. Show that you care by anticipating their needs, being empathetic, and delivering your services with authenticity. By putting your clients first and demonstrating a genuine interest in their success, you'll build strong, lasting relationships that will serve you well throughout your career.

As a seasoned recruiter with over 44 years of experience, I've learned many valuable lessons throughout my career. One that stands out is the importance of genuine concern for your clients and how it can make all the difference in securing a significant Placement.

Early in my career, I was working with a cutting-edge airframe manufacturer looking to fill a crucial role in their engineering department. They needed a lead engineer with a unique blend of technical expertise and leadership skills to oversee the development of a new aircraft design. It was a challenging position to fill, and the client was growing increasingly frustrated with the lack of suitable candidates.

The hiring manager and I had a basic working relationship, and the opportunity with this company had huge potential. I decided to pay them a visit to see if I could better understand the engineer's frustrations.

Now, I'm no engineer—far from it, in fact. But within a few minutes meeting with the man who would oversee this position, I felt his pain. I readily understood the pressure he was under to get it right the very first time. He needed a special kind of person in this job. An engineer who understood it was more than just a job. Lives were at stake, tens of thousands of workers' jobs depended on these designs being perfect. The entire corporation and all of its shareholders would not tolerate a single failure.

I went back to my office with a much clearer understanding of the candidate they needed. Soon after, I came across some interesting information on a brilliant engineer named Michael. He had an impressive background, having worked on several groundbreaking projects in the aerospace industry. However, he was currently employed by a smaller company and hadn't considered making a move.

I reached out to Michael and took the time to understand his career goals and aspirations. I learned that he was eager to take on a more significant leadership role and make a lasting impact in the industry. I knew he would be a perfect fit for my client, but I also recognized that leaving his current company would be a significant decision for him.

I worked closely with Michael, providing him with detailed information about the opportunity and the company culture. I also took the time to address his concerns and answer any questions he had. I genuinely wanted to ensure that this move was the right one for him, not just for my client.

When I presented Michael to my client, I didn't just focus on his technical qualifications. I emphasized his leadership potential, his passion for innovation, and his dedication to his craft. I also shared my insights into his character and how he would fit into the company's culture.

My client was impressed with Michael's background and the level of detail I provided. They appreciated the fact that I had taken the time to find a candidate who not only met their technical requirements but also aligned with their values and vision.

In the end, Michael was offered the position, and he accepted it with enthusiasm. He went on to lead the development of a groundbreaking new aircraft design, which solidified the company's position as a leader in the industry.

This experience taught me the importance of being genuinely invested in both your clients and your candidates. By taking the time to understand their needs, concerns, and aspirations, you can make more meaningful connections and ultimately drive better outcomes for everyone involved. It's a lesson I've carried with me throughout my career, and it's one that I believe is essential for any successful recruiter.

7 MARKETING CALLS

There is a general consensus among Big Billers that telephone marketing is THE KEY to their success. And I think most of us who have a few years recruitment experience do acknowledge that fact. So, why do I constantly read about 'alternative' (read that as 'easier') approaches to marketing? Does our continuing love affair with all things electrical and computer-driven really help us that much? Or is it because we managers and educators have forgotten how to correctly teach our business? I think it is a combination of all of the above. With this in mind, let's look at how to build an effective marketing campaign and make a successful telephone marketing call.

The Human Voice

Some years ago, I read in a promotional piece which IDC put together to discuss new phone systems that "Voice communication is, and will continue to be, the most valuable part of the communication ecosystem, especially in the enterprise. With all the hype surrounding convergence, content, mobility, and multimodality, the single most powerful application that unifies and clarifies all forms of communications is the sound of the human voice."

The intro continued, "With its ability to add context through tonal subtleties, plus the ability to glean feedback in real time, voice has an advantage that is practically unbeatable when compared to other forms of communication. When communicating with family and friends, voice is the first choice and provides an intimate sense of connection that cannot be conveyed in an email or IM session. For example, voice can relay concern from a grandparent or express the joy of a newfound relationship that goes beyond the meaning of the words used in the conversation. The demands on resources and time also amplify the value of a voice conversation."

In recruiting, the subtleties achievable in voice communication allow us to establish rapport. That is, our clients and our candidates must like us, believe us, trust us and understand us. Once that happens, we can influence their behavior. But keep this in mind…you can't establish rapport through keystrokes. No matter how often you tweet or how many folks write on your Facebook wall, the human voice wins every time!

Why Market

A free economic marketplace is constantly correcting itself. While some companies fail, other companies will rise to take their place. Some win. Some lose. And so, we market on a daily basis to 'vector in' on the winners because they are the ones who need our Placement services. And often, we find some of our best candidates among the losers—the companies that are downsizing, experience lay-offs, or simply going out of business. In a sluggish economy where there are more companies failing, Big Billers might double or triple their marketing activity to find the few companies that are flourishing. But they continue to find them!

Now, we can't call everyone in the world, so the Big Billers figured out that you need to set parameters around your specialty—to delimit your niche. Since, no matter how 'marketing challenged' we are, most of us can make 25 marketing call connects in one 8-hour workday.

Now, just multiply it out: 25 connects per day equals 125 per week; equals 500 per month; equals 1500 per quarter. So, **'1500' became the magic number.**

Once we determine those 1500 client contacts, we want to recycle these folks four times per year. Then, based on the 4% Placement rule, we will place with 4% of the 1500 or make 60 Placements per year; multiple that 60 by an average fee of $10,000 and you have your $600,000 yearly desk; multiple that 60 by an average fee of $20,000 and you now have your $1,200,000 yearly desk. It's all in the numbers.

Of course, in this difficult economy, there are not so many of these top billing desks anymore—at least not as many as in the past. There are two reasons for this:

First, most of us don't make nearly the number of calls that I just suggested. Then we compound that error when, after stumbling on what we consider a workable job order (JO), we immediately stop marketing (something we were not in love with anyway) and start recruiting on the new JO—because recruiting is so much more fun!

Second, the 4% rule fluctuates—unfortunately, sinking in a tough economy—so today it is probably below 4%, but probably above 2%. The numbers and ratios also change with the individual recruiter. One set of numbers does not make a 'universal.'

Choosing Your Vehicle

I came out of a system that encourages the use of a Most Placeable Candidate (MPC) as the vehicle they recommend weaving into their marketing presentations. This system's MPC approach contributed to its growing into the world's largest, and most profitable, contingency recruitment firm—a title they still own to this day! Obviously, their marketing approach works.

The MPC usually possesses five qualities: They have a marketable skill, are realistic about everything—title, salary, commute, etc., are reference-checkable, will interview when you say and start within 2 weeks, and exhibit mutual respect with the recruiter. Once we identify this individual, who admittedly is hard to find, we can prepare to attack our marketplace, but first we need to have something to say, and this is where the FAB comes into play.

The FAB

Here's an overview of the Feature-Accomplishment-Benefit presentation—the FAB. The definitions are:

Features—Facts about the candidate.

Accomplishments—Significant 'measurable' results the candidate obtained for their current and past employers. These are 'concrete' and can consist of numbers, fractions, dollars and/or percentages.

Benefits—Educated guesses of what the candidate can do for a new employer based on their accomplishments.

The Target of Your Call

I am often asked how 'contingency' recruiters can act more like 'retained' recruiters. I always answer the same way, "ACT more like retained recruiters." Retained recruiters always 'enter' a company at the highest level. This means, if you want to be treated like a CEO, you need to call at the President/CEO level. A critical rule of thumb to remember is: You will always be treated at the level you penetrate a company. If you penetrate at the CEO level, you will be treated like a CEO and will receive JOs at the VP level and below.

A critical rule of thumb to remember is: You will always be treated at the level you penetrate a company. If you penetrate at the CEO level, you will be treated like a CEO and will receive JOs at the VP level and below. If you penetrate at the VP level, you will be treated like a

VP and will receive JOs at the Director level and below. If you penetrate at the Director level, you will be treated like a Director and will receive JOs at the Manager level and below. If you penetrate at the Manager level, you will be treated like a manager and will receive JOs at the 'worker bee' level and below. And if you penetrate at the HR level, you will be treated like a clerk. When you complain that you are being treated like a clerk, it is because you are acting like a clerk. Sorry, these are just the recruitment 'facts of life.'

The Triplicate-Triplicate Entrance to the Call

OK, you now have your MPC and your FAB presentation. Now it's time for the rubber to meet the road. No more delays. IT'S TIME TO MARKET! And it's time to meet the Gatekeepers.

Every 'Gatekeeper' is eventually going to ask you the same three questions:

1. What's your name, or who are you?
2. What company are you with?
3. What is the nature of your call?

So, you might as well address this (using the first Triplicate) by answering these three questions before they are asked.

1. "My name is Bob Marshall."
2. "I am with TBMG, International in Atlanta, Georgia."
3. "And I am actually calling for three reasons."

Now you go into your second Triplicate.

1. "First, I am calling to introduce myself to the CEO."
2. "Second, I have something of a confidential business nature to discuss with him/her."

3. And finally, "I have just recruited a top-notch candidate who ..."(go into your FAB, if appropriate).

At this point, you can get your first objection from the Gatekeeper who might say, "Oh, you are a recruiter. You need to talk to Tom in Personnel or Sally, our In-house Recruiter."

You say, "OK, I will. What is that extension? Now can you pass me through to the CEO, because, you see, I still want to introduce myself to him/her, and I still have something of a confidential nature to discuss with him/her." By the way, these confidential items can include the name of your MPC and, of course, your fee/guarantee agreement.

Don't be surprised if your response takes the Gatekeeper by surprise. You will be the first recruiter who agrees with the objection, yet still asks to be put through to the person you were calling in the first place. This will be confusing to the Gatekeeper. But after he/she collects himself/herself, they just might put you through.

Even if you get voice mail, the key is to make sure that the CEO hears your voice when you record your message and makes the connection to what you do. You might not be successful on this call, but remember, you are going to call this CEO four times per year. Eventually, you will get through.

The Call

Bob: "Hello, is this John Hopkins? John, you are the CEO of IGT, aren't you? Terrific! John, my name is Bob Marshall. I am a recruiter in the Atlanta area, and I called you for a couple of reasons. First, I wanted to meet you over the phone. And second, by way of introduction, mention to you that I have just recently surfaced a top notch sales talent (Feature) who last year developed a brand new territory into one of the top five producing territories out of 200 in the country for his current company—one of your competitors—(<u>Accomplishment</u>) and there is no reason why he can't bring that talent to bear with a new company like yours (<u>Benefit</u>). This candidate has been asked to relocate and wants to stay, if possible, in the Atlanta area, and so I am calling local companies to determine interest and also to introduce my recruiting service. John, if you would like to talk to my candidate, I have arranged for him to be available next Monday morning or Tuesday afternoon. Which one of those days would be good for you or would you like more information about him?" (<u>Close</u>) (60 seconds elapsed time)

> John: "We have no openings."

Bob: "Oh, I guess I didn't make myself clear. I am a recruiter. I would venture a guess that 90% of the companies I place with don't have openings when I call but do want to be kept apprised of top notch talent as that talent surfaces. One of the reasons for my call was to see if you wanted to provide yourself and your company with this unique service." (20 seconds)

> John: "Well, that's fine, Bob, but we just don't have any openings."

Bob: "OK, but let me ask you two more questions and then I will let you go. First, which companies do you suggest I call with this sales talent in mind? (indirect marketing call) (10 seconds)

> John: "Well, you could call Lift Engineering and Lion Manufacturing."

Bob: "Great. And second, what kind of person would you like to hear about should I uncover that person in a subsequent search (this is the Lost Sale close—see below). Remember, I am a contingency recruiter, so that means that it costs you nothing to look at my candidates. Only if you make them an offer and they accept and start to work does my service charge come into play." (20 seconds)

John: "If you ever have a director of engineering, I would definitely want to talk with you."

Bob: "OK, John. It was a pleasure speaking with you!" (2 seconds)

John: "Thank You."

The Exit From the Call

After you have utilized your Triplicate/Triplicate approach, and then made your FAB presentation with no effect, you now need a graceful and profitable exit from your marketing call. So, let's say this call is going nowhere, and you are ready to get out of this presentation and on to your next presentation. Before you leave this hiring manager, say this, "OK, I understand that you have no openings right now, but let me ask you one last question. What kind of person would you like to hear about should I uncover that person in a subsequent search?" We call this the 'Lost Sale' approach. You are not selling anymore. You have given up.

You are symbolically waving the White Flag. But, before you go, you are going to ask for information to help you sell this hiring manager on your next marketing call. Your next call can now be more precise, more targeted, and more successful.

The Goals of the Call

I believe that the main goal of the marketing call is to engage the other side in conversation and to reach the magic 2-5 minute window where rapport building takes place. Less than two minutes and the call is not long enough for rapport building; over five minutes and you run the risk of not being able to call all of the companies you need to call in order to recycle 1500 per quarter. Don't get me wrong. I like the idea of arranging a Send Out for my MPC, but also want to start the rapport building process: fashion optimum length conversations, avoid the 'no openings' objection, and obtain alternate Job Orders and additional 'client needs' information I can utilize down the road.

There's your effective marketing presentation. Do 25 of these per workday...doctor's orders!

Now let's go write some Job Orders. *But* let's make sure they are workable before we start recruiting on them.

8 PAINKILLERS

DAN WAS ONE OF MY GOOD FRIENDS AND MENTORS IN THIS industry; he was a unique recruiter. As a master of our business, he was superb in so many ways, and he taught me so much. One of the techniques he is famous for is entitled the 'I Have Arranged. . .' approach.

Dan once told me that he had a 100% Presentation to Send Out ratio on his matching calls. In other words, a JO pre-exists, and you are calling back the Hiring Manager to present a candidate for the opening. Most of us run a 25 to 50% hit rate on this call, but Dan, AKA 'Robocruiter,' was at 100%. How is this possible?

Robocruiter said that most of us make a fundamental mistake when we initiate the call: we fail to requalify the JO and/or set the stage for the subsequent interview. We just call in and present our candidate. At the end of our breathless monologue, we hear the Hiring Manager say, "Gee, he really sounds good, Bob. Send me his resumé." Or, "Well, I don't know, let me think about it and I will get back to you." So, we have basically arranged nothing. This isn't quite fair when you consider that we were given the job order, or search assignment, with the expectation that it was an urgent matter. We already won once when we wrote the Job Order. Based on that victory, we then went to our marketplace and expended a lot of time and effort (for free if this was a contingent assignment) betting that anyone we would find would be a match. And now we have received nothing for our hard work. Woe is us!

But Robocruiter approached this task a little bit differently. First, after he had recruited his candidates, he would call the HM and re-qualify the JO.

"John, remember when you gave me the information on this search assignment you said that the title of the position was 'X'. Is that still the same? Yes? Well, that's good. And that the duties and responsibilities were 'Y'. Has that changed at all? No? Good. And that the salary range was 'Z'. Is that still the same? Good. And that you agreed to pay my 30% fee. Are we still OK there? Good."

Then he would set the stage.

"Then I have some good news for you. I have canvassed the area. I have talked to many potential recruits. And finally, I have refined the list down to three who are qualified and are good matches for you and your company."

Then he would set the hook.

"So, John, this is what I have done. *I have arranged* for these three recruits to be available to speak with you next Monday and Tuesday (as we had pre-agreed) at 9, 10 and 11. Now let me tell you a little more about them."

Robocruiter always presented his candidates to his client companies in this way. He first re-qualified the JO, he then set the stage, and finally, he inserted the 'I have arranged' close. His central focus was that he had *arranged* for those people to be there. In his mind, it was a done deal, because it had already been arranged.

This approach works for a couple of reasons: hiring managers, and indeed most businesspeople today, have things arranged for them. So, what you're doing is fitting into that nice, neat package of how they do business anyway. Also, if something's arranged, the implication is that it's going to take place. Consider these two invitations: "Let's have lunch sometime while you're in town," versus "I have arranged for us to have lunch at noon on Wednesday at Ruth's Chris." Which do you believe? With the latter, it's arranged.

You can actually picture Ruth's Chris restaurant and can even visualize the table where we will be sitting. It's done. As opposed to saying, "Let's have lunch sometime," which is an ambiguous invitation that will never happen.

The 'I have arranged' approach works. Try it and you will see. And just like Robocruiter, you, too, will attain a 100% SO to Presentation ratio when you call back your Hiring Managers on the Job Orders you have already written.

9 QUALIFYING THE JOB ORDER

A STUDENT OF MINE CALLED THE OTHER DAY. HE HAD SPENT all week conducting a concentrated marketing campaign and had written a few new Job Orders. He was now using my Job Order Matrix system to qualify his JOs, but it was taking him what he thought was an inordinate amount of time. He asked if there was a shortcut in the JO qualification process. I asked if he had ever heard of the Qualifier Job Order approach, and he had not. And so, we began to talk about this Big Biller technique.

0-1 out of 15

You may already be familiar with my presentation entitled, "Your Desk as a Manufacturing Plant," (*coming up in the next chapter*) when a top recruiter writes fifteen Job Orders, they will usually fall into three distinct categories:

- 0-1 will be of 'Search Assignment' quality;
- 4-5 will be of the 'Matching' type; and
- About 10, or 2/3rds, will be of the 'Can't Help' variety.

The Qualifier Job Order

In general, recruiters seem to naturally possess a 'positive mental attitude.' Because of this PMA, they think that every Job Order they write is of Search Assignment quality—that it's supremely 'fillable.' While it may be necessary to have a positive outlook, we need to temper it with a strong dose of reality.

Let's use the example of Ricky Recruiter's new marketing campaign. Ricky makes marketing call after marketing call with no positive results. Then, out of the blue, one of his phone calls reaches a Hiring Manager who actually seems to like Ricky and is willing to talk with him—and, surprise of surprises, actually is looking to fill a critical need and is open to giving Ricky some JO information. At this point, Ricky is so elated that he keeps the poor HM on the phone way too long. It's only human nature.

But keep this in mind. This HM was not expecting Ricky's call. Combine that with the fact that most of us are nice people, and you start getting a sense of the beginning of Ricky's downfall. Blindly moving forward, Ricky takes his time and fills out all of the empty blocks on his Job Order form. When he finally hangs up, he runs to his manager and says, "See, everything I write is a Search Assignment." Or, Ricky might tell his manager 'The Big Lie.' It goes something like this: "You know, Mr. Manager, you keep telling me to make a lot of marketing calls—and I am fine with that. But every JO I write is a true Search Assignment. I have more Job Orders on my desk now than I can possibly fill. What I need to do is recruit." And that's what he will do—to the exclusion, I might add, of any further marketing activity. His downfall is now complete!

The Big Lie

Now, why does our industry fall into 'The Big Lie' trap? Because the assembled, unqualified Job Orders on your desk are, for the most part, garbage. You are working in areas where you are not going to be paid and then, at the end of the day, you can't understand why you have no/low production. You criticize the industry or your manager or anybody but yourself. But what has really taken place is that you haven't properly qualified your Job Orders so that you can be assured of subsequent successful Placements. What you have done is wasted time.

Think of the rest of the scenario. Think of what happens when the HM finishes his long initial call with Ricky. He turns to his secretary and says, "You know, it never dawned on me while I was talking to this guy, but he's a Recruiter. He took a lot of my time asking me questions about our company that he could have found the answers to by doing a little Internet research. And he actually wants me to pay him a fee to find someone for us. Can you imagine that? I mean, we can run ads, our personnel people can find that kind of person. I tell you what, the next time he calls, tell him we moved to Peru. Or better yet, that I'm in a meeting and can't be disturbed. I don't want to talk to him anymore. He's already wasted my time, and I'm just not that interested."

Now, you see, you have two opposite points of view of the same situation. The Recruiter, who thinks he has a Search Assignment, is going to spend the next three weeks recruiting on it, while giving up his marketing campaign. And the HM has just given specific instructions to his secretary not to let this person in anymore. Well, if that's going to happen, let's find out the first day, before we have expended any more of our straight commission time on it.

The Qualifier Job Order (JO)

What you are going to do when writing a Job Order is get six pieces of information. After those six pieces of information are secured, you are going to look at your watch and say, "Gee, how time flies. I must leave for an appointment. However, I need more information from you. Can I call you at 3 pm this afternoon; or would 9 am tomorrow be better? I'll need about 20 minutes of your time."

At this point, you put the JO aside and continue making your marketing calls.

The Six Pieces of JO Information

1. Contact Information

Name of the company, address, name of the HM, title, secretary's name, phone numbers—all of the regular pieces of 'contact' information.

2. Duties and Responsibilities

You need to know a day in the life, a week in the life, or a month in the life of the position. Or, what are the percentages of supervisory time, of technical time, and of administrative (paper shuffling) time that equal 100% so that you can find the Candidates who match those percentages.

3. Salary and Fee

You're going to need to know the low, medium, and high salary range (we don't discuss these amounts with our recruits). Also, you're going to need to discuss your service charge at this time and cover it in both dollars and percentages so that you can be sure that the HM understands what they will need to pay you.

4. The Hiring Process

Here is where you qualify for urgency. You are going to say, "When is the last day that you can keep this position open without something bad happening the next day if it is still open? In other words, what is your 'drop dead' date?"

You don't ask the question, "When would you like this person on board?" That question doesn't define urgency. What you want to know is the last day. If they say to you, "Well, we're not going to hire until we find the right person," what you have just determined is that this is probably a 'can't help' situation. Because that means they can go indefinitely with the position open. Or if they say, "Well, it's a new position. We just don't have any time constraints on it." Again, probably a 'can't help' JO. What you want to do is get a specific date to establish urgency.

You also want to ask about the length of their hiring process, who else interviews, how many interviews are required, and when the decision will be made. What you are doing here is nailing down the hiring process timeline so that you will be able to determine later if the process goes off plan. You are setting the parameters.

5. The Recruitment Column

You want to find out who they want, what three or four companies, or competitors, they respect and want someone from, or what industry they want people from. You can then go out and 'Rifle Shot' recruit— extract people precisely for this position in the least amount of time.

When you ask, "Who do you want for this position?" if they missed that you are a Recruiter going in, they are now going to know that you are a Headhunter because you are actually asking for a 'head to hunt.'

Sometimes Recruiters say to me, "But Bob, if they knew who they wanted, they could go out and get that person themselves." But what those Recruiters don't understand is that there are a lot of reasons why HMs can't, or won't, recruit on their own. They can't do it because they don't have the talent to do it. They put themselves in jeopardy by trying to take someone from a competitor because they could start an employee poaching war. Or they risk starting a salary escalation war. A lot of HMs don't take people from their competitors because they don't want to be rejected. They run the risk of getting into an interview situation (where proprietary information is given) and then being rejected. Now that information can be taken back to the original competitor, with disastrous effects. These are just a few reasons why our client companies will use Recruiters and give that Recruiter the exact name of the person they want to fill the position.

6. The Personality of the HM

What schools did that person attend? What are their interests or hobbies? Let's say that the HM's major hobby is fishing for sharks. He actually dives into the water, catches the sharks with his bare hands (and a sharp knife)! I guarantee you that if you find a Candidate, not even a technical match, who jumps in the water and kills sharks by stabbing them with a knife, you are going to get a hire. In your introduction, you might say, "Mr. HM, I know you wanted an EE, but I've uncovered an Industrial Engineer that you will be interested to know not only is terrific at what he does, but also has the same hobby as yours." Bottom-line is that you are going to get a hire, and it wasn't even for the position for which you were searching. Always keep in mind the personality matches. They are absolutely critical. Too often, we work and work making the best technical matches in the history of western civilization, and we never find out the chemistry or the personalities of the two parties. And we put people together who mix like oil and water, i.e., they don't! And when we don't get the Placement, we wonder why. Sometimes it's because we weren't aware of what was going on behind the scenes. We didn't think past the technical match.

The Call Back

You now have the six critical pieces of information—your skeleton JO. Now set the times for your call back, say goodbye and hang up the phone. Continue with your daily plan. At the agreed upon time (be exact here), call the HM back. If he answers your call, that is the first qualifier that this is a good JO. Please note that you have done nothing on this JO up to this point. You don't want to waste your time on an unprofitable venture. The 'Call Back,' and having the HM actually talking to you on the phone again, now allows you to determine more clearly if this is a fillable JO.

Now, there are three ways to call back:

1. Call back that afternoon, or the next day, to write the complete JO. You should allow only a short time to elapse before you call the HM back.

2. There are Recruiters who, when they call back, present a 'File Search Candidate.' This will be a close match—not an ideal one—who they pulled from their files. The purpose here is not to get the person placed or even set up an interview. What they want to determine is how the HM reacts when a Candidate is presented. Again, to determine urgency and to determine the integrity behind the HM working with the Recruiter.

3. Some Recruiters are so current on the talent that they have previously recruited, that they can actually make presentations to the HM while they are taking the Qualifier JO. This is more unique, but it is a way to 'test the waters' and find out how the HM reacts when ideal Candidates are presented. This is very prevalent in the Sales specialty areas.

This is a quick way to start the JO qualification process. And another technique from the Big Billers.

Now that we know which JOs to work, let's start doing a little recruiting.

10 YOUR MANUFACTURING PLANT

I want to share a powerful framework that has helped countless recruiters understand and optimize their business. It's called 'Your Desk as a Manufacturing Plant,' and it's an analogy that breaks down the key components and processes of a successful recruiting operation.

Imagine you're a new recruiter, setting up your desk for the first time. You're now the General Manager of your own manufacturing plant, which we'll call "Rapport Builders Incorporated." Your goal? To build strong relationships with hiring managers and candidates by making them like you, believe you, trust you, and understand you.

As the GM, you'll be overseeing the production of two main products: job orders and candidates. Job orders come in three flavors: 'search assignment' (the crème de la crème), 'matching' (solid, fillable orders), and 'can't help' (the bottom of the barrel). Candidates also fall into three categories: 'most placeable' (your stars), 'matching' (good, but not great), and 'can't help' (back-burner material).

Now, a manufacturing plant can't run with a GM alone. You'll need to hire some key players:

1. The Production Manager - Responsible for churning out quantity —job orders and candidates, day in and day out.

2. The Quality Control Manager - Tasked with sorting job orders and candidates into their proper categories based on quality.

3. The Sales Manager - The master matchmaker who arranges Send Outs (interviews) and chases down decisions.

4. The Controller - Your trusty number-cruncher who keeps you grounded in reality.

Every day at 4:00 PM sharp, you'll convene a meeting with your team. You'll grill the Production Manager on quantity, the QC Manager on quality, the Sales Manager on Send Outs and decisions, and the Controller on profitability. If anyone's slacking, it's time for a pink slip.

But here's the key to keeping your operation humming: recycling. Don't toss those 'can't help' job orders and candidates in the trash. Situations change, so run them through your recycling plants and see if you can upgrade them to 'matching' or even 'search assignment' quality.

To survive in any economy, you'll need about 1500 company contacts to hit that sweet spot of 25 marketing connects per day. Touch base with them once a quarter on average and watch those relationships blossom.

Ratios are your secret weapon. Out of every 15 job orders, expect 1 unicorn, 4-5 solid matches, and 10 duds. Same goes for candidates. Armed with this knowledge, you can allocate your time and energy where it counts.

Send Outs and decisions—that's where the magic happens. Aim for two quality Send Outs a day, and remember: a decision is a yes, a no, or another interview. No maybes allowed.

If you find yourself in a slump, don't panic. Odds are, it's either your Production, Quality Control, or Sales Manager that needs a tune-up. Identify the weak link and make targeted tweaks instead of overhauling your entire operation.

Block off sacred time for your 4:00 pm powwow and morning marketing blitz. Let your subconscious work its magic overnight and come in fresh and full of ideas.

Above all, make rapport-building your north star. Even if you don't snag a Send Out or Job Order on every call, a small victory in rapport will keep you dialing with a smile.

Master this manufacturing mindset, and you'll be well on your way to top-producer status. It's not about being perfect—even a minor league tweak can yield major league results. So, fire up that plant, rally your team, and let's build some rapport!

11 SMALL CAN BE BIG

I think one of the most striking statistics I have come across in my recruitment career was that historically a whopping 70% to 80% of all new jobs came from small (1-49 employees) and medium-sized (50-499 employees) companies. That's a massive chunk of the employment pie that a lot of recruiters are probably overlooking.

It reminds me of a story from early in my career. I had just landed a retained search with a household-name tech giant, and I was feeling pretty cocky. I figured filling the role would be a slam dunk—after all, who wouldn't want to work for a company like that?

But as I started reaching out to potential candidates, I kept hitting walls. The comp wasn't competitive. The interview process was a bureaucratic nightmare. And most of the top talent I approached was already happily employed…often at smaller, more nimble firms I'd never even heard of.

It was a humbling experience, but it taught me a valuable lesson: never underestimate the allure and opportunity of small and mid-sized companies. What they may lack in brand recognition, they often make up for in spades with things like:

- Faster decision-making and shorter hiring cycles
- More competitive compensation packages
- Greater opportunities for impact and advancement
- Tighter-knit, more engaging company cultures.

Of course, as some rightly point out, working with smaller companies isn't without its challenges. Cash flow can be an issue, so it's important to vet their financial stability and potentially structure deals with that in mind. And while they may have less red tape, they also have less robust HR infrastructures, so more of the hiring process may fall on your shoulders.

But in my experience, the pros far outweigh the cons. When you build relationships with growth-stage companies and become their go-to talent partner, the opportunities are endless. You're not just filling a req—you're helping to build the team that will take their business to the next level. That's incredibly fulfilling.

Plus, I've found that smaller companies are often more open to creative staffing solutions, like contract-to-hire arrangements or volume discounts for multiple Placements. They're less set in their ways and more willing to try new approaches if it means getting the talent they need quickly.

One strategy is to use larger companies as sources of candidates versus clients. (*Why do you think all of those recruiters are located in Seattle...think Boeing and Microsoft!*) It's a smart way to fish where the fish are, so to speak, without getting bogged down in all the hoops and hurdles of their hiring processes. Cherry-pick the best talent from the big boys, and then place them into high-impact roles with up-and-coming contenders. It's a win-win.

Therefore, to all the recruiters out there who are limiting their outreach to Fortune 500 firms, I'd say this: think small to make it big. For every requisition you see from a mega-corporation, there are dozens more waiting to be discovered at the SMBs driving the majority of job growth. Seek them out, nurture those relationships, and watch your Placement rates soar.

Because at the end of the day, it doesn't matter if your candidate is coding the next killer app from a garage or a glittering Silicon Valley campus. As long as you're making matches, making an impact, and making money, you're winning the recruitment game. And as the data clearly shows, the smart money is betting on small.

Part 3 | Growth Strategies

"The future belongs to those who learn more skills and combine them in creative ways."

- ROBERT GREENE

12 THE 12 PRINCIPLES

I already introduced you to David. He found me by reaching out to legendary editor Paul Hawkinson at one of the premier publications in our industry, "The Fordyce Letter."

My time with David was spent teaching him recruitment techniques based on the 'Twelve Principles.' that top producers possess:

For your interest, we focused on the following twelve principles that top producers possess:

1. They stay on the phone more often than not; usually double to triple the time of the average biller.

2. They make each call with higher quality, not because they are smarter, but because they get more practice by doing it more often.

3. They know they will be successful; they expect success. When they make a Placement, they instantly use that excitement and get back on the phone. They use that excitement to make more calls with a higher success rate. They get in the ZONE.

4. They delimit their marketplace by having borders; they identify 1500 company contacts in their chosen niche and call those contacts every quarter (25 calls per workday). They want to selectively handpick the 4%, or 60, who they will develop as clients and with whom they will place.

5. They always know their numbers and ratios.

6. They always market to get new blood, new business, and to hone their marketing skills.

7. They always treat this business as a process, and not as a series of events.

8. They always plan the previous day and have an MPC (Most Placeable Candidate) ready to market, so that they can hit the ground running the next day.

9. They know when to turn down a Job Order and not waste their time.

10. They have a lot on their hot sheet (at least 5 full deals); they are not dependent on any one deal at any given time.

11. They implement 'The Theory of Threes'; this is taking three candidates to three companies and arranging three Send Outs with each company—or a total of nine Send Outs—thereby tripling their chances for success.

12. They are focused on the right activity. They are disciplined. They know that all deficiencies come down to two areas: either a knowledge deficiency or an execution deficiency. They know how to fix either. They strive for consistency. They know their actions become their habits.

That is our foundation. So, now that we know who we are, we can move on.

13   THE PERFECT RECRUITER

Picture this: you're a manager at a recruiting firm, and you've just met a bright-eyed, bushy-tailed recruiter candidate who seems to have that special something. But how can you tell if they've got what it takes to be a top producer?

First things first, let's talk about the essential qualities every recruiter needs to bring to the table. We've mentioned it before. We're not looking for Mensa members, but they've got to be sharp. Creativity is key—each call is a new adventure, and they need to be able to think on their feet. Corporate maturity is a must, even if they're fresh out of college. Tenacity, self-motivation, and a balanced life outside of work round out the nonnegotiable.

Beyond that, there are some 'Nice-to-Haves': a track record of success in the face of adversity, a touch of positive hostility, a good sense of humor, empathy, a healthy ego, persuasiveness, active listening skills, decisiveness, intuition, a knack for planning, and natural leadership abilities.

I remember one recruiter I hired early on in my career. She was a former high school teacher with zero sales experience, but she had this incredible energy and a genuine passion for helping people. Fast forward a year, and she was consistently billing in the top 10% of the company. It just goes to show that raw talent and the right attitude can take you far in this business.

Okay, you've found a promising candidate. Now it's time to give them the lay of the land. I like to use the doctor analogy. Just like a physician, we recruiters are experts in our field. We have a process, and we need our clients (and candidates) to trust us and give us the information we need to make the perfect match. It's all about building rapport and establishing ourselves as trusted advisors.

Training is where the rubber meets the road. You can teach skills all day long, but if your new hire doesn't have the right attitude, it's all for naught. That's why I'm a big believer in cultivating a positive mental attitude from day one.

I once had a recruiter who started off strong but hit a slump a few months in. He was putting in the hours but couldn't seem to close a deal. We sat down and realized he'd lost sight of why he got into recruiting in the first place—to change lives for the better. We started each day with a quick motivational session, reading testimonials from happy clients and candidates. Within weeks, his numbers were back up, and his passion was reignited.

Of course, even the best recruiters can get burnt out. That's where retention comes in. Studies show that money is the top motivator for account executives, followed by autonomy and challenging work. As managers, it's on us to create an environment that feeds those needs while providing support and guidance.

One of my favorite retention strategies is the 'Directors' Club'—a periodic incentive trip/money for top performers, given to their significant others who they declare as such when they come on-board. Not only does it give them something to shoot for, but it also fosters camaraderie and friendly competition among the team. Plus, a little R&R never hurt anyone's production and the significant others love it!

At the end of the day, being a Big Biller boils down to a few key things: a winning attitude, laser focus, meticulous control of the process, unwavering discipline, and a dedication to putting relationships first. Master those, and the sky's the limit.

Bo Schembechler: 'Leadership'

All of us can find reasons to complain. No matter how idyllic scrolling through others' social media feeds, life is rarely picture-perfect. We might wish it was, but what do we accomplish by complaining? Nothing.

Let me recount a story about what happened at the University of Michigan and revolved around the football team, their legendary coach, Bo Schembechler, and their new team co-captain, a young inside linebacker named Andy Cannavino.

It seems that the 1980 Michigan Wolverines football season started in tough fashion. After three games, their record was one win and two losses. Not a good opening for one of the strongest football programs in the United States.

One day an assistant coach came into Bo Schembechler's office and mentioned that there was some complaining by many of the players. It was being said that Michigan practiced too long and hit too hard during those intense practices. The players also said that that was why the season was starting so poorly. Bo asked the assistant coach who was making those comments. The assistant said that many players were guilty, but that it was also coming from the team captain. Bo said, "That's interesting! Get him in here." Bo was not one to wait when problems surfaced.

Now the Captain, Andy Cannavino, was a big strong kid. He came into the office, and Bo recounted what the assistant had said. Andy admitted that he had indeed said those things. At that point, Bo said, "The University of Michigan has had a long and illustrious football history. Since I have been the head coach here, we have always had tough practices because football is a tough game. I would like you to tell the captains of teams gone by that you think our practices are too long and that we hit too hard. I would like you to complain to them. Do you know what they would say to you? They would tell you that you are a bad team captain, Andy Cannavino, and they would be right. On the field, you represent me. And as the coach on the field, you are letting me, your teammates, and the whole program down."

At that point, with a tear flowing down his cheek, Andy Cannavino understood Bo's message and that he needed to lead by example. He said, "I understand, Coach. There won't be any more problems." And there weren't. Under Andy's guidance, the team straightened themselves up. There was no more grumbling or complaining. The team finished the season by winning all the rest of their games and playing, and winning, in the Rose Bowl—not something that the University of Michigan did all the time. Andy Cannavino was acknowledged as the greatest team captain in Michigan's history.

One insightful CFO I knew used to say that if a choice in your life is 80% positive, jump all over it, because nothing is 100%. And yet, sometimes I hear grumbling and complaining in the offices where I train. Sometimes I hear it from the managers. And sometimes I even hear it from those in upper management at the various corporate headquarters. Remember, we are either going to be part of the solution, or we will remain part of the problem. I encourage everyone to take a page out of the University of Michigan's football history and be positive. Be strong in your conviction that we belong to the best industry of its kind in the world. Trust that all of us are trying to do our best and that we truly do care for one another. Carry that with you as you return to your desk and pick up your telephone and watch the winning tradition you will build!

This is the inside scoop on finding, hiring, training, and retaining the total account executive. It's not always easy, but when you see your team crushing their goals and changing lives in the process, it's worth every ounce of effort.

14 NAVIGATING INDUSTRY CYCLES

Mike Crosswell, during the late 1990s, was the owner of Blue Arrow, the UK's largest privately-owned staffing organization.

I met Mike at that time when he was on the Board of Advisors of the same company who had relocated me from San Diego to Atlanta to become their VP of Corporate Development (Trainer). We had offices around the US, but also in the UK, Malta, and Cyprus. It was my duty to travel to those offices and train the recruiters and managers.

One night when I was in London, Mike and I had dinner at the Hilton Langham Hotel, near Oxford Circus. We started talking about this and that, and eventually, since this was December, our conversation turned to Goal Setting & Planning for the New Year.

I asked Mike how he did this at Blue Arrow. Mike told me that he had too often seen recruitment organizations let their coming year's goals be set for them by their individual recruiters instead of by upper management. In other words, the goal commitments were coming from the 'bottom up' instead of from the 'top down.' By definition, this is what is referred to as an example of 'Undercut Management.'

Mike explained that at Blue Arrow they decide at Corporate what they want their total revenue to be for the coming year. Then they sit down and look at all of their offices and the revenue flow histories of each. Based on this information, a portion of the total revenue goal is assigned to each office. He compared it to cutting up a big apple pie.

When this procedure is finished, the individual office managers are assigned their target goals for the coming fiscal year. Each manager is then asked, "Can you attain that number?" If they answer "Yes," then the goal is set in concrete. If they answer "No," or say that they are not sure, this follow-up question is asked, "What can we at Corporate do to ensure that you will hit this number?" It's as simple as that.

After all of this is settled, the managers return to their offices and divide up their number and assign portions to each of their recruiters in much the same way as the managers were assigned their office number by Corporate. At this point, the manager asks their recruiters the same two questions that they had been asked. In this way, they get an office-level commitment to their expected revenue goal for the year.

At the end of this process, the manager not only knows what support they can expect from Corporate to help their office reach their goal, but they will also know what their recruiters expect to help guarantee their individual numbers. By using Mike Crosswell's format, Blue Arrow constantly hit their goals and eliminated year-end surprises.

This was the simple brilliance of Mike Crosswell and one of the reasons why he was so successful while running Blue Arrow. His sage advice is as clear to me today as it was on that special night so many years ago in foggy London.

15 AHOY, MATE! CHANGES AHEAD

You know your niche. Better than that, key players in your niche know you. It's a natural fit, and you can't imagine running your business in any other segment.

Let me share with you a cautionary tale—the story of the whaling industry. Yes, we have to go back a ways for this one, one hundred and fifty years to be precise. Whaling was a booming business, with the United States leading the charge. We owned more whaling ships than the rest of the world combined, and the industry contributed a staggering $10 million (in 1880 dollars) to the GDP, making it the fifth largest industry in the United States. But within the span of just 50 years, the entire industry was dead, our active whaling fleet had fallen by 90 percent, and the industry's real output had declined to 1816 levels.

What happened? The answer is simple: new, better, cheaper forms of energy were being introduced. Oil, gas, and eventually electricity rendered the whaling industry obsolete. Just like that, a once-thriving industry found itself without a purpose, and those who had built their careers on it were left stranded, their skills and expertise no longer in demand.

Think that example is unique? Think again. Throughout history, numerous upheavals have led to radical shifts in the economy and workplace.

Some notable examples include:

1. **Industrial Revolution** (late 18th to 19th century): The shift from manual labor to mechanized manufacturing dramatically changed the nature of work and led to urbanization, as factories replaced small-scale workshops.

2. **Advent of the automobile** (early 20th century): The rise of the automotive industry transformed transportation, manufacturing, and labor markets, leading to the growth of suburbs and the creation of new jobs.

3. **World War II** (1939-1945): The war effort led to significant advancements in technology, manufacturing, and women's participation in the workforce, setting the stage for post-war economic growth.

4. **Digital Revolution** (late 20th century): The widespread adoption of computers and the internet transformed communication, commerce, and the workplace, leading to the growth of new industries and the decline of others.

5. **Globalization** (late 20th to early 21st century): Increased international trade, outsourcing, and the rise of multinational corporations have reshaped the global economy and labor markets.

6. **Sharing economy and gig work** (early 21st century): Platforms like Uber, Airbnb, and Freelancer have disrupted traditional industries and changed the nature of work, with more people engaging in flexible, short-term contracts.

7. **COVID-19 pandemic** (2020-2023): The global health crisis has accelerated the adoption of remote work, e-commerce, and digital technologies, leading to significant changes in consumer behavior and the workplace.

These are just a few examples of the many upheavals that have transformed the economy and the nature of work throughout history, each leading to the rise of new industries, the decline of others, and significant changes in the way people live and work.

Now, consider the recent emergence of Generative AI, with the release of ChatGPT and its various counterparts. This technology has the potential to revolutionize the way we work, just as oil and gas did for the whaling industry. Suddenly, tasks that were once the domain of highly skilled professionals can be accomplished with the help of AI. And just like the whalers of old, many of the IT professionals who have enjoyed a decade of prosperity and job security may find themselves facing a similar fate.

According to the World Economic Forum, Artificial Intelligence and other economic drivers will result in 83 million job losses over the next five years—a staggering 46% of the workforce. That means that nearly half of the jobs we know today could be rendered obsolete in the span of just three years.

What does this mean for you, the aspiring recruiters of tomorrow? It means that you must be prepared to adapt, to embrace change, and to seek out new opportunities. You cannot afford to become complacent in your niche, thinking that the way things have always been done will continue to work.

Instead, I encourage you to explore new specialties and skillsets that are emerging in the wake of technological innovation. Learn how to leverage AI as a sourcing tool and discover the new niches that are opening up as a result of the changing landscape.

Remember, the whaling industry thought it would last forever, but it was ultimately undone by the very forces that it had once dominated. Do not let that be your fate. Stay ahead of the curve, be proactive in your approach, and never stop learning and adapting. The future may hold challenges, but it also holds incredible opportunities for those who are willing to seize them.

16 BUILDING YOUR PRACTICE

LET'S TALK ABOUT TWO CRUCIAL CONCEPTS THAT CAN MAKE OR break your success in this wild and wonderful world of recruiting: building your practice, or as we used to say, 'Desk Building, and Inverted Cones'.

First up, desk building. This is where you get to let your imagination run wild and pick a specialty that gets you so fired up, you can't wait to jump out of bed each morning and dive in. Maybe it's a field you already know inside and out, so you can hit the ground running. Or maybe it's something totally new that you can't wait to learn all about.

I remember when I first started out, I was drawn to the fast-paced world of tech recruiting. I spent hours poring over industry blogs, attending conferences, and picking the brains of anyone who would talk to me. It was a lot of work, but by the time I made my first Placement, I felt like I could hold my own with even the most seasoned engineers.

Once you've settled on your specialty, it's time to get granular. Read every trade publication you can get your hands on. Scour job boards to see which roles are in high demand. And here's a pro tip: find the biggest, juiciest job ad in your niche and make it your personal mission to fill that role.

But don't just start randomly calling people—be strategic. Put on your detective hat and do some serious sleuthing to find the ideal candidates. Tap into your network, scour LinkedIn, and don't be afraid to get creative. The goal is to cast a wide net and reel in as many qualified candidates as you can.

And here's where the magic happens: on every single call, you need to be a master multitasker. You're not just recruiting—you're also marketing, gathering intel, and planting the seeds for future Job Orders. It's a delicate dance, but when you nail it, the payoff is huge.

Okay, now let's talk about inverted cones. Picture two cones lying on their sides, pointing in opposite directions. The one on the left represents your specialty, and the one on the right represents your target market.

When you're just starting out, your specialty is going to be pretty broad, and your market is going to be pretty narrow. Let's say you're focusing on finance roles in the Chicagoland area. For the first few months, you'll be calling every bank, investment firm, and accounting office in the Windy City, trying to get a feel for the lay of the land.

But as you start to gain traction and build relationships, you'll naturally start to narrow your focus. Maybe you realize that there's a ton of demand for internal auditors, so you start to specialize in that niche. At the same time, your market starts to expand—now you're getting Job Orders from companies all over the Midwest.

Fast forward a year or two, and you're the go-to recruiter for internal audit roles in the manufacturing industry. Your specialty is razor-sharp, but your market is massive—you're working with companies from coast to coast and even overseas. Congratulations, you've reached the promised land of recruiting: the power broker stage.

But here's the thing: markets can change on a dime. One day you're riding high on a wave of Job Orders, and the next, crickets. That's why it's so important to be nimble and adaptable. If you find yourself in a dry spell, don't be afraid to back out of your niche and try something new. It might feel like starting over, but trust me—all that expertise you've built up will serve you well no matter what specialty you pivot to.

Master these concepts, and you'll be well on your way to recruiting rock-stardom. But above all, remember to stay curious, stay hungry, and never stop learning. In this business, the only constant is change—and the recruiters who thrive are the ones who are always ready to adapt and evolve.

17 ALIGNMENT WITH YOUR GOALS

If we work together, one of the first things I am going to do is have you tell me why you are in this business. Yes, I want to know about your business, but how you tell your story will let me know a great deal about you. Now, how much of you is an integral part of your business?

I lean back in my chair, taking a sip of coffee as you outline your vision for the new professional services startup. The passion in your voice is palpable—it's clear this is more than just a business venture for you. It's a calling, a chance to make a real impact in the world.

"That's what I love to hear," I say with a nod. "But before we dive into the nuts and bolts of recruiting top talent, I want to take a step back. Have you given much thought to your company's mission statement? Its core values and guiding principles?"

You furrow your brow, and I can see the wheels turning. "Of course," you reply after a moment. "We want to provide top-notch consulting services that drive real, measurable results for our clients. And we're committed to doing it with integrity, transparency, and a relentless focus on innovation."

I nod slowly. "Those are all well and good, but they're just words on a page if they're not backed up by action. A true mission statement isn't just a marketing ploy—it's a moral compass that guides every decision you make, big or small."

Leaning forward, I fix you with an intense gaze. "Let me ask you this: if you had to choose between landing a lucrative contract with a company that possibly engages in less than ethical business practices, or walking away from that deal, what would you do?"

You don't even hesitate. "Walk away, every time. Integrity has to come first, no matter what."

A smile spreads across my face. "Exactly. That's the kind of unwavering commitment I'm talking about. When your recruitment strategies are firmly rooted in your core values and overarching mission, everything else falls into place."

I take another sip of coffee, letting my words sink in. "It's not just about finding the best talent—it's about finding the right talent. People who share your vision, your passion, your uncompromising standards. Because at the end of the day, your employees aren't just cogs in a machine. They're the beating heart of your organization, the ones who will make or break your success."

Pushing back from the table, I rise to my feet. "So, as we move forward and start mapping out your recruitment game plan, keep that mission statement front and center. Use it as a filter to weed out candidates who might be technically skilled but culturally misaligned. Because when you've got a team that's truly bought into your vision, that's when the magic happens. That's when you can achieve things that go far beyond just turning a profit."

I extend my hand, and you grasp it firmly, a newfound determination burning in your eyes. "You've got the passion, the drive, and now, the roadmap. I can't wait to see where this journey takes you."

Now, this approach works with your clients. Employers crave people who can share their vision. It also applies to you in your recruiting business (or whatever business you are in). Have a vision for your firm that mirrors the direction of your life. If you've found your 'True North,' add that to your business model, refine it as needed, and look for others who can share in that passion.

18 MARKETING 101

A BRIEF DETOUR. MANY YEARS AGO, I WAS A YOUNG MAN stationed overseas with the Navy. On one occasion, I had the chance to observe flight operations up close and personal. I remember watching the flight deck of this massive ship, watching in awe as F4 Phantoms screamed overhead, their engines roaring like thunder.

One by one, they would approach the carrier, lining up with the flight deck and gradually descending until they snagged the arresting wire with their tailhooks. It was a ballet of precision and power, a dance on the edge of disaster.

Picture this: you're that fighter pilot, hurtling through the sky at breakneck speeds. Your mission? Land your jet on a tiny strip of pitching flight deck in the middle of the ocean, all while battling wind, waves, and the relentless pull of gravity.

What strikes me most was the intense focus and concentration etched on the faces of those pilots. Even from a distance, you could see the way their eyes narrowed, their jaws clenched, their entire beings locked in on the task at hand. And who could blame them?

Landing a 30-ton jet on a pitching, rolling, heaving deck in the middle of the ocean is no small feat. The margin for error is razor-thin, the consequences of failure catastrophic.

I remember chatting with a grizzled old Air Boss after one particularly hairy landing. "How do they do it?" I asked, my voice tinged with equal parts admiration and incredulity.

That Air Boss grinned as he fixed me with a steely gaze and held up four fingers. "It's all about the details, son. Airspeed, altitude, line-up, and the 'meatball.' Focus on those four things, and you'll make it home every time."

Sound impossible? Not if you focus on just four things. We overcomplicate tasks to the point they become untenable. Focus on the essentials.

That lesson stuck with me long after I traded my Navy blues for civilian clothes. And it's a lesson that applies just as much to the world of recruiting as it does to the world of naval aviation.

Now, what does it have to do with marketing calls? Everything, as it turns out. Just like that ace pilot, a top-performing recruiter needs laser-like focus and unwavering concentration to succeed in the high-stakes world of talent acquisition. In this fast-paced, hyper-connected age, it's all too easy to get thrown off course. Constant interruptions, digital distractions, and the siren song of social media can derail even the most seasoned recruiter. But as the saying goes, 'In the absence of clearly defined goals, we become strangely loyal to performing daily trivia until ultimately, we become enslaved by it.'

Now, how do you stay on target and avoid the tyranny of the trivial? By zeroing in on the four pillars of recruiting success:

1. Maintaining a robust pipeline of Job Orders and candidates
2. Crafting compelling marketing presentations
3. Properly qualifying opportunities and talent

4. Prioritizing high-probability assignments

Simple? Yes. Easy? Hardly. But just like flying a jet, mastering these fundamentals is the key to reaching rarefied heights of performance.

Of course, even the most skilled recruiter can fall into a slump from time to time. When the job orders dry up, and the candidates ghost, it's tempting to blame external factors like the economy or the competition. But, more often than not, a dip in production can be traced back to one of three internal culprits: lack of activity, poor quality control, or inadequate deal-closing.

The solution? Get back to basics. Dial up your marketing intensity to uncover fresh opportunities. Sharpen your qualifying questions to weed out tire-kickers and time-wasters.

And brush up on your closing techniques to turn Send Outs into Placements. But here's the thing: all the skills and strategies in the world won't save you if your head's not in the game. Attitude is everything in this business, and it's one of the few things completely within your control.

I once heard a story about a Russian dissident who was sentenced to hard labor in the gulag. Every day, he toiled in the frigid cold, sustained by little more than a crust of bread and the hope of survival. And yet, as he lay shivering in his bunk each night, he would think to himself, 'Today was a good day.' He had a roof over his head, food in his belly, and the promise of another chance tomorrow—and for that, he was grateful.

Now, I'm not saying we should compare the challenges of recruiting to the horrors of a Soviet prison camp. But the lesson is clear: mindset matters. You can choose to focus on the frustrations and setbacks, or you can choose to embrace the opportunities and possibilities. The power is yours. So, the next time you pick up the phone to make a marketing call, remember the four things that fighter pilot focused on to land safely on the deck.

Remember the Russian dissident who found a reason to be grateful in the darkest of circumstances. And remember that success in this business comes down to the four things you can control: your attitude, your activity, your skills, and your planning.

Master those, and you'll be flying high in no time. And who knows? You might even develop a taste for hard things. As JFK once said, "We choose to go to the moon...not because it is easy, but because it is hard."

Here's my challenge to you which I may repeat more than once: choose the hard things. Choose to make that extra call, to refine that presentation, to go after that tough-to-fill order. Not because it's easy, but because it's hard—and because that's where the magic happens.

19 HOW TO ACQUIRE THE RIGHT ATTITUDE

I caught myself staring out the window at the front pasture so icy and desolate in the late winter afternoon. It had been cold lately...unseasonably cold for Atlanta. And, with the vanishing warmth, I started having negative daydreams. Was this economy ever going to recover? Did our political leaders really know what they were doing? Was recruitment, as I had known it, a thing of the past, like typewriters and Polaroids? Sad thoughts. And then, as always, the phone rang.

I returned to the present and answered the phone. Another like soul was full of some of the same doubts I had just been having. But it was his question that shook me out of the doldrums. He asked, **"What is the difference between success and failure in recruitment?"**

This took me back to a meeting I had in Atlanta with one of the greatest sales trainers who ever lived. His name was Steve Brown, and he was the Chairman of the Board of The Fortune Group. I told the caller to sit back and relax and listen to what I remembered from that memorable meeting—the meeting where Steve explained to me how salespeople acquire the Right Attitude.

First let's remember the three major differences between Big Billers and average billers, with an emphasis on point number three:

1. Big Billers do what average billers do, but they do it more often;
2. Big Billers do what average billers do, but they do it with higher quality;
3. **Big Billers do what average billers do, but they have a better attitude; in other words, they believe they are going to be successful, when average billers are just not sure.**

Number three is the key point. As Steve Brown would say, "The difference between success and failure in sales is attitude."

Attitude

Over the years in my career, even though I am considered a 'nuts and bolts' type of trainer, I have been lucky to associate with some of the great sales trainer motivators of all time. I grew up in recruiting listening to Tommy Hopkins and J. Douglas Edwards, flew with Zig Ziglar from Atlanta to Dallas, heard Cavett Roberts in person and Dr. Leo Buscaglia on videotape, and had a day-long meeting with Steve Brown, who is recognized by many as one of the foremost sales and management trainers in the world.

When I lived in San Diego, Lou Scott, an icon in the industry, arranged for me to meet up with Steve Brown during an Atlanta stopover on my way to Nashville to do some recruiter training. Steve and I met in the morning over breakfast, and then he took me over to his headquarters and introduced me to his staff. I spent a full day with Steve watching him in action and how he interacted with people. He was brilliant.

And upon leaving, he gave me an autographed copy ('for Bob Marshall who knows the thrill of Training. Steve Brown') of his book "13 Fatal Errors Managers Make* And How You Can Avoid Them" and his seventeen module training program entitled "Creative Selling Skills."

Based on that meeting, and my own personal 'take' on the subject, let's consider this topic of Attitude—how to get it and how to keep it.

As soon as we start talking about attitude, we face our first hurdle. "Attitude" seems to be one of the most over-worked words in selling. How many times have you and I heard that we must have a Positive Mental Attitude in order to be successful? Believe me, we recruiters hear it so much that we either:

1. Stop hearing it (tune out), or
2. Become rebellious.

But think of it a different way. Any true professional's real secrets to success are their highly trained skill and ability, which will lead to the right attitude. A doctor will tell you this—or a lawyer, an engineer, the captain of an ocean liner.

The mistake we make in recruitment is that we try to magically acquire this Positive Mental Attitude. Well, it is a proven point psychologically that the more we try to force an attitude into the mind, the more the mind rejects it. The bottom line is that positive attitudes are not acquired by willpower.

How Attitudes are Acquired, Changed, or Modified

Attitudes are acquired, changed, or modified in two ways, and two ways alone:

1. Change in environment or conditions (temporary)

If I can change your environment severely enough, I can change your attitude. If I can magically put $1,000,000 into your pocket, once you realize that change, your attitude will completely change.

On the other hand, if I can change your conditions adversely, I can also change your attitude. If I can magically transport you, moneyless, to a strange country where you don't know anybody and you do not speak the language, once you realize that change, your attitude will also change completely.

Implementing this theory, when a recruiter hits a slump, how do we change their environment or conditions? We tell them to work harder, suggest longer hours or change their desk location. We give them a new candidate to market or even suggest a new specialty niche—anything so that they will have a chance to feel more successful and be able to sell more successfully.

The only problem with this approach is that we are 'manipulating' attitudes, and that won't last for an extended period of time.

2. Acquisition of ideas or knowledge (long-lasting)

Ah, yes…this is the long-lasting solution because the knowledge becomes a part of you. Through knowledge, attitudes have sources, and you will have the ability to return, when necessary, to your sources and the knowledge you have acquired. This is where the trainer enters the picture with new training ideas, daily planners, quick resource guides, and videos or webinars.

Ours is a unique profession. Most of us got into recruitment after pursuing some other endeavor. Most of us didn't go to college or university to get a degree in recruitment. But, for whatever reason, we ended up in this fascinating profession. And then, right away, our manager, or some trainer, told us that we needed to have the right attitude in order to be successful. As a result, we started to force that attitude in our mind.

Now, don't get me wrong. While a positive attitude is critical, most professionals have it because they have spent a lifetime acquiring knowledge that causes that attitude to naturally be there. If their confidence ever gets low, they don't go home and look into a mirror and try to force themselves to have the proper attitude. They merely return to the knowledge they had previously acquired.

Therefore, those of us in selling need to follow the same path as any true professional. We need to have the ability to revisit our sources of knowledge.

The Right Attitude is comprised of two elements:

Enthusiasm and Self-Confidence.

Enthusiasm

What are the two sources of enthusiasm?

1. Product Knowledge (knowing what we are selling); this involves a detailed understanding of the specialty area in which we recruit and the candidates who populate that area.

2. Knowing what we can do for others (knowing the miracles we can perform for our clients and candidates, how we can help them), we change lives for the better, on a daily basis. We help both our client companies and our placed candidates to become more successful quicker.

But occasionally, even the best recruiter loses their enthusiasm for their desk. Why do they lose their enthusiasm?

They become exhausted, worn out. If this happens, they need to take a couple of days off, relax, play golf, go fishing.

Or they become too accustomed, or hardened, to what they can do for others. It gets to be 'old hat.' Get in the habit of conditioning your thinking so that you can go back to what you can do for your clients and your candidates.

On every day of your selling lives, have a personal sales meeting—something that includes motivational literature; maybe a testimonial letter from a satisfied client or candidate. Read these over aloud for the animation to help get the words into your subconscious (that's the nine-tenths of your brain that controls your behavior).

Self-Confidence

What are the three sources of self-confidence?

1. Product Knowledge

You need to know your specialty niche and the companies and candidates who live there. You need to know the lexicon of your specialty.

2. People Knowledge

You need to know the answers when your client, or your candidate, asks you a question. Remember, we are always looking for candidates who can make an impact on our client companies—either Superstars (candidates who can make our clients' money) or Heroes (candidates who can save our clients' money).

3. Recruitment/Selling Skills Knowledge

Here is the foundation that any good trainer will lay out for you. These are the tools of our trade—the MPC, the FAB, Sales Linkage, the Qualifier JO, the Eight Point Candidate Prep, etc. You just need to learn them and then use them daily. Treat your recruitment profession as a 'process' and not a 'series of events,' and you will be consistently successful.

Don Miguel Ruiz

In past articles, I've briefly mentioned a little book with profound advice. This is a book entitled "The Four Agreements" (A Toltec Wisdom Book) by Don Miguel Ruiz.

In the beginning of his book, Don Miguel says that we didn't get to choose our beliefs, but that they were handed down to us from our ancestors who learned these beliefs from their ancestors. Then our ancestors passed that information; whether right or wrong, on to us on how to live and how to dream (he calls this our 'domestication'). But when that information is faulty, how can we change it? Don Miguel gives us the solution to this dilemma when he covers the four agreements that can move our attitudes in a more positive direction. Here they are:

1. Speak with integrity; take responsibility for your actions; don't judge.

Every client and candidate is looking for an honest recruiter. I don't know one Big Biller whose success is based on telling fibs. They are all 'straight arrows,' and their clients and candidates respect their integrity. As my favorite CFO once told me, "If you treat people with honesty, that honesty will be returned to you. And if you treat people like crooks, they will start acting like crooks."

2. Don't take anything personally; become immune to the opinions of others.

The Big Billers don't read their press clippings and don't rely on others to establish their sense of worth. They know that they are great producers and simply act that way. And, as Robocruiter always said, "I never take rejection personally. It is simply a refusal to do business with me at any given point in time, and I can live with that."

3. Don't make assumptions; always ask questions; communicate clearly.

Big Billers ask a ton of questions and learn from the answers they receive. They always ask one question at a time ('unbundling') and wait for the answer before asking their next question. They know that the person asking the questions always controls the conversation. And they practice the questioning technique of Rudyard

Kipling who, when asked how he became such a great writer, said, "I had six guides that taught me everything I knew. They were 'what' and 'when' and 'where' and 'how' and 'why' and 'who.'"

4. Always do your best; avoid self-judgment, self-abuse, and regret.

In the words of one of my favorite people to quote, Anonymous, "Successful people aren't born that way. They become successful by establishing the habit of doing things unsuccessful people don't like to do. The successful people don't always like these things themselves; they just get on and do them." Always do your best and you will end your journey with no regrets.

It is my belief that, if you make those four agreements, and blend them with the sources of enthusiasm and self-confidence, then you can't help but attain, and own, the Right Attitude forever. Then your sad daydreams will disappear. You will realize that the economy will recover, that our political leaders will see the light, and that recruitment, as a profession, will never disappear from our economic landscape.

20 CLIMBING THE MOUNTAIN

Now let's talk about the lifeblood of your business: landing new clients. Because let's face it, no matter how great you are at recruiting, if you don't have a steady stream of new clients knocking on your door, you're going to be in trouble.

I had the chance to view the movie "Meru" about mountain climbing, but this was not just another movie about Mount Everest. It was totally different. And as with most things in my life, I thought about how it was analogous to what we do as recruiters.

So, let me digress for just a minute and tell you about the conquering of Meru, the 'anti Everest.' The critics say that Jimmy Chin's documentary on scaling the Shark's Fin may be the best climbing movie of the year, only it's not really about the climb.

The allure of Meru peak and its Shark's Fin climbing route is simple. The mountain, a 21,850-foot jagged monster in India's Garhwal Himalayas, is believed by Hindus to be the center of the universe. The Shark's Fin, a 1500-foot vertical rock wall at the very top is considered one of the hardest climbs in the world, with no Sherpa team to set ropes, no bustling base camp for support. And no international notoriety; Meru climbers call it the anti-Everest.

In 2008, Jimmy Chin, Conrad Anker, and Renan Ozturk set out to climb the nearly featureless granite wall of Shark's Fin. At the time, no one had ever completed the ascent. After 20 days in extreme conditions, the group gave up just 300 feet from the summit. Three years later, after Chin vowed to never set foot on the mountain again, the team regrouped and set out to tackle Shark's Fin and film Chin's attempted ascent.

"Meru" premiered at the 2015 Sundance Film Festival. Ultimately, the film is less about mountain climbing than it is about loyalty and obsession and friendship. A film that told a powerful story about universal ideas that people could relate to. Climbing is an incredible vehicle to tell that story.

"I'm incredibly fortunate to have a great mentor. Does it feel scary sometimes, yes, but there's deep devotion and a lot of attention to detail. I think it's lost on a lot of people how complex the decision making is and how sophisticated it is when you're making decisions with your life, the stakes are so high. Meru is one of the great challenges of Alpine and big wall climbing, and nobody has ever even heard of it.

"Only a small community within our climbing community even really understands what that mountain is, and that itself makes it.an anti-Everest because no one knows it. But the climbing is also extremely difficult. It requires a high level of competency in every type of climbing: mixed climbing, ice climbing, snow climbing, rock climbing, aid climbing. It requires you to have a very solid quiver. And it's not mountaineering. It's high altitude, big wall climbing.

"There are no places on Meru where you can put a tent down. You have to live in portaledges hanging there. There's 1000 feet of the route that are totally overhanging. And unlike Everest, you don't have a giant Sherpa team. Putting the ropes up for us. So that we could zoom up the rope. We're carrying everything we need on our backs."

It was a terrific movie, and I recommend that you check it out. I want to share several points that are Meru-centric as opposed to those that are Mount Everest related, and I hope you will now be able to appreciate the difference.

Preparation is Key: Success in business, as in climbing, requires meticulous preparation. Understanding the landscape, equipping yourself with the right tools, and having contingency plans can make the difference between success and failure.

Resilience and Perseverance: Overcoming setbacks is part of the journey. The ability to bounce back from failures, learn from mistakes, and persistently pursue goals is crucial for long-term success in any business venture.

Adaptability: The business world, like the unpredictable conditions of a mountain, can change rapidly. Being able to adapt strategies, pivot when necessary, and remain flexible in the face of change is essential for survival and growth.

Teamwork and Trust: Achieving ambitious goals requires a team that works well together, trusts each other implicitly, and supports one another through challenges. Building a strong, cohesive team is fundamental to accomplishing complex business objectives.

Vision and Goal Setting: Clear goal setting and having a vision are pivotal. Like climbers setting their sights on the summit, businesses need to have a clear objective and a strategic plan to reach their pinnacle of success.

Risk Management: Understanding and managing risk is vital. Just as climbers assess their routes and potential dangers, businesses must identify, evaluate, and mitigate risks to ensure sustainable progress and safeguard their ventures. These lessons underscore the parallels between the discipline required for climbing and the strategic, mental, and emotional preparedness necessary for navigating the business world.

The Importance of a Renewable Client Base

Now, take all of those lessons and translate them into gaining new clients. Think of your client database as a garden. If you only focus on the plants that are already growing, eventually, they'll wither away. But if you're constantly planting new seeds and nurturing them, you'll always have a bountiful harvest.

That's where the three strategies I'm about to share with you come in. These are the same techniques used by the best of the best in our industry, the true 'Meru climbers' of recruiting. By implementing these strategies, you'll be able to consistently add new clients to your roster and break free from the feast-or-famine cycle that plagues so many recruiters.

Strategy #1: The 12-Month Rotating Marketing Call Mastery Touch Plan

The first strategy is all about staying top-of-mind with your potential clients through a systematic, multi-touch approach. Here's how it works:

1. Determine your specialty niche size (aim for about 1,500 potential clients per quarter).

2. Recycle these contacts four times per year via phone and eight times per year electronically.

3. Use a mix of marketing calls, boilerplate emails, industry-specific articles, blog posts, event invitations, and more to keep your name in front of your niche.

Remember, the key here is consistency and variety. By reaching out to your potential clients through multiple channels on a regular basis, you'll establish yourself as a trusted expert in your niche and be the first person they think of when a hiring need arises.

Strategy #2: The Client Referral Plan

The second strategy is all about leveraging the power of referrals. As the old sales adage goes, "The best source of new business is a happy client." Here's how to turn your satisfied clients into a referral-generating machine:

1. When clearing your fee, ask for two promises: agreement to pay your fee and agreement to provide introductions to five colleagues in their niche who could use your services.

2. Never forget a customer, and never let a customer forget you. Stay in touch, show appreciation, and report results.

3. Strike while the iron is hot. Follow up on referred leads within six minutes, not six days or six weeks.

By making referral-gathering a standard part of your process and consistently nurturing your client relationships, you'll create a virtuous cycle of new business that will keep your pipeline full and your billings high.

Strategy #3: The Client Direct Mail Plan

The third strategy is a bit of a throwback, but don't underestimate its power: direct mail. In a world of overflowing inboxes and constant digital distractions, a well-crafted piece of physical mail can really stand out. Here's how to make it work:

1. Send out ten handwritten notes with a business card and a stamp per day (2,640 per year).

2. Expect a 6-7% return rate (that's 185 more positive responses than you're getting now).

3. Use direct mail to soften up your next phone call or email and make the phone ring. By combining the personal touch of a handwritten note with the consistency of a monthly mailing campaign, you'll differentiate yourself from the competition and create a sense of 'stickiness' with your potential clients.

Becoming a Trusted Advisor

Now, I know what you might be thinking: "This all sounds great, but how do I find the time to do all this on top of my regular recruiting duties?" And that's a valid concern. But here's the thing: by establishing yourself as a trusted advisor in your niche, you'll actually save time in the long run.

When your potential clients view you as an expert, they'll be more likely to take your calls, respond to your emails, and give you the inside scoop on upcoming hiring needs. You'll be able to uncover those hidden Job Orders that never get posted and beat your competition to the punch.

And that's really what it's all about, isn't it? Being the recruiter that everyone in your niche knows, likes, and trusts. The one they can't imagine not working with. The one who does the things that others only dream of.

Conclusion: Climbing Your Meru

So, are you ready to climb your own recruiting Meru? To do the things that other recruiters only imagine and become the go-to expert in your niche?

It won't be easy. It will require consistency, creativity, and a lot of hard work. But the view from the top will be worth it.

By implementing these three proven strategies for landing new clients—the 12-month marketing plan, the client referral system, and the direct mail campaign—you'll be well on your way to building a renewable client base that will sustain your business for years to come.

And remember, as the great Frank Bettger once said, "If you take care of your clients, they'll take care of you." So go out there and start planting those seeds. Your bountiful harvest awaits!

21 CONVERSATION WITH A SUPERSTAR

Wisdom of 'Robocruiter' and the Total Account Executive, Part One

RECRUITABLE JOS

When we market, we will uncover three distinct types of JOs: Search Assignment (SA), Matching, and Can't Help JOs. This is a 'given;' it is indisputable, and we must recognize that fact. If a superstar writes 15 JOs, 0-1 will be of SA quality and recruitable; 4-5 will be matching and semi-recruitable; and 10, or 2/3rds, will be of the Can't Help variety. So, the $64,000 question is: How do you determine which JOs are which? And which are recruitable?

Recruitable JOs – Qualities

1. Total and complete information, uniqueness, HM bios—Develop qualities about the JO that make it unique, that give it sizzle. We are going to recruit candidates who are happy, well-appreciated, making good money and currently working, and we need something that we

can use to entice them to make a move. Stay away from 'vanilla' JOs. Also, it is critical that we get HM biographical information. Most Placements contain a significant amount of chemistry matching—and this is how we initially find out that information.

2. Cooperation – The HM needs to see you as an equal, not as a forced irritant that he must deal with temporarily. Every client-candidate-recruit relationship is equal on all three sides.

3. It must be urgent; they must be ready to hire NOW—we need a 'drop dead' date. If there is no deadline to fill, then there is no urgency. And if there is no urgency, our job becomes very, very difficult and highly problematic.

4. Commitment for semi-exclusivity – Semi-exclusivity (including retainer formats), show that the client has 'skin in the game.' This is good for us and usually smooths out the process.

5. No resumes – Resumes are in the portfolios of job hoppers, job shoppers, and rejects. We find candidates who, as a rule, don't have these. By the HM requesting a resume, it only slows down the process. At the very least, stay away from starting the process with a resume. Use a Statement of Match (SOM) instead. Then, after the telephone or face-to-face interview is arranged, you can send all the resumes your heart desires.

6. Hiring Process qualified – Who interviews, when and where, the time between interviews, the time from the last interview to the hiring decision—all of this is critical information, and very professional for you to ask for and for you to know. This needs to be agreed upon at the beginning of the relationship. These are the rules of the game. If you don't do this at the beginning, you don't have the right to do this at the end.

How to Qualify the JO

I actually witnessed Robocruiter qualify his Job Orders when I visited his office. This is what happens:

Robocruiter will stop the HM in the middle of taking a JO and say, "I think I can help you, but let me explain to you how I work." When the HM says that they have worked with recruiters in the past, Robocruiter says, "Well, that's fine, but you have never worked with me, so let me explain the difference.

Number One: My service charge is 30% of realistic first year's earnings. It's not negotiable. My time is as valuable as the next guy's—and I'll need your OK on this today because this will be the last time we will talk about that.

"Number Two: I offer a 30-day guarantee. If the candidate doesn't start to work, I will refund the service charge and, if he is terminated, or quits, in the first 30 days, I will credit my service charge toward the candidate's replacement—and I'll need your OK on this today because this will be the last time we will talk about that.

"Number Three: I recruit people who are happy, well-appreciated, making good money, and currently working, and I entice them to move for a better opportunity (i.e., yours, if you give me the appropriate information to conduct the search). I will not present you job hoppers, job shoppers, or rejects—those who are looking at the electronic 'want ads' on the Internet. What this all means to you is that I won't have resumes, or C.V.s. Don't ask me to send you one because it will only slow down the process and possibly cause you to miss the opportunity of interviewing my highly qualified and desirable candidates while they are available—and I'll need your OK on this today because this will be the last time we will talk about that.

"Number Four: All offers need to come through me. I serve the function as a buffer and as an ombudsman during the offer process. Being utilized in this way, I can almost guarantee that an appropriate offer will be accepted—and I'll need your OK on this today because this will be the last time we will talk about that.

"Number Five: I will need to take an in-depth Job Order. This means that we will need to set up a time for me to call you back for this activity to take place—and I'll need your OK on this today because this will be the last time we will talk about that.

"Number Six: I will need to arrange a time, after the interview, to share with you the candidate feedback. Because you and I are both busy businessmen, we will need to set up an agenda for this post-interview meeting so that it can proceed quickly—and I'll need your OK on this today because this will be the last time we will talk about that.

"Number Seven: I will need to be able to contact you in a timely manner and will need your home phone number should the need arise to reach you after hours. Also, we will need to prearrange a time when we can talk (should the need arise) on a daily basis—and I'll need your OK on this today because this will be the last time we will talk about that.

"And Number Eight: I will ensure that your Return-On-Investment (ROI) will be in your best interest for the long run. Is all of this clear?"

He says this in a nice, matter-of-fact, way.

The Five Reasons Why AEs Don't Close

1. They don't feel entitled to close, because they haven't made a commitment to the business and so never got the information necessary to close at the beginning of the relationship.
2. They sometimes agree with the employer's excuses to delay rather than the recruiter's need to get a decision.

Unfortunately, 'Time Kills All Deals.' The more delay, the more likely this situation will not come together for us.
3. They fear losing something—usually caused when they don't have a full hot sheet (*interviews in process*). We all need five full situations or ten splits on our hot sheets in order to guarantee our success.
4. They have a hard time hearing "No." We need to teach our recruiters that this is not rejection, but a refusal to do business. It's not personal; it's just the way business is conducted.
5. People, by their very nature, are wishers and hopers. We sometimes think that if we wish and hope hard enough, our deals will come together. And sometimes that happens, but this is not a sound business strategy.

The 13 Motivational Paths

1. **You have to want to be motivated** – We need to realize that people do things for their own reasons, not yours. Motivation comes from within.

2. **Find out what motivates you and do it** – Robocruiter used to always say, "If it is to be, it is up to me."

3. **Volition, or willpower**, to continue to pursue the goal no matter what – Of the five qualities we look for in AEs, tenacity seems to stand above the rest. Aesop's fable of the tortoise and the hare comes to mind here.

4. **A continued plan for learning** – When we stop learning, we regress. All of the Big Billers I know are great students and eager learners.

5. **Single out success stories** – Remember your successes and relive them. These attributes will anchor positive thoughts in your

subconscious. 90% of your brain consists of the subconscious. It believes what you tell it—whether positive or negative—you choose.

6. **Use motivational recordings** – Again, positive thoughts beget positive thoughts. Stay away from the news media, in any of its forms. They are, by their nature, negative and de-motivating.

7. **Set the example** – Be enthusiastic. It's contagious. We learn best by modeling behavior.

8. **Advance into new markets, retainers, etc.** – While implementing the 'classics,' stay on the cutting edge of what we do.

9. **Listen and talk to the new AEs** – The new people need us the most. They want the reinforcement that they are doing a good job and that they are doing it correctly.

10. **Keep up to date in your industry** – Know what's happening in your niche. Become a Power Broker.

11. **Focus on end results** – Don't focus on the individual acts that get you to the end result, just focus on the end result.

12. **Differentiate between being 'up' and being 'on'** – You can only be 'on' for short periods of time. You can be 'up' much longer.

13. **Goal set** – As a rule, professional and business goals will lead to personal goals. These are the benchmarks that guide our progress.

The Things You Will Lose by Implementing These Techniques!

In conclusion, keep in mind that those of you who will take this information to heart and strive to become the Total Account Executive, will lose some things with this concept:

- You will lose frustration;
- You will lose incompetency;

- You will lose wasting time on assignments that you should not be working on in the first place;
- You will lose continuous 'blank' months;
- And, you will lose the tendency to 'burn out,' because things that you most enjoy, you never burn out on! (Just try to stop eating for a while.)

22 CLOSING AND CLOSES

THE PHONE RANG. WHEN I ANSWERED, THE CALLER WAS anxious. He was very close to putting a deal together but was stuck in the hiring process. I suggested he go into a 'Negative Yes' closing sequence. He didn't know what that was. I said, "OK, then let's try a 'Ben Franklin Balance Sheet' instead." He didn't know that one either. And finally, I said that was OK as well, just to remember the 'Reduce to the Ridiculous' if the salary objection came up again. He didn't know that one either. And so, I ended the call by scheduling a time when I could teach him the traditional Sales Closes.

Packaging

I believe that Selling and using Closes is merely telling the truth in an attractive manner. Now, before I start discussing these sales 'packaging' techniques, I need to reaffirm that 'sales' is not a dirty word. In my mind, it is merely more attractively packaging our candidates and Job Orders. I am not advocating trying to talk people into doing something that they truly don't want to do, nor into anything that is not in their best self-interest to do. It is merely packaging. It is an attempt to bring the advantage to our side. Think of it this way: When I am giving you a gift, I can toss it to you unwrapped and say, "Here's your gift," or I can carefully wrap it in pretty paper and put a big bow on it and gently present it to you. Which gift do you think has the greater value? I contend it is the one that I wrapped. Think of Closes in this way. They are gift wrapped. And we are Salespeople, and Salespeople use Closes.

Closes

When I teach Closes, I want you to know where they come from and how to use them in your business. It's important to learn how to use them on every phone call and in every sentence. That's why the great sales trainers teach the ABCs: Always Be Closing.

Closes are used to structure your conversations. Like a guide, you should know where you want to go. You just need to take your prospects with you. Closes are the tools you use to amplify your chances of success. And you use many and diverse closes every day. You don't want to be caught short-handed. In my opinion, one of Abraham Maslow's greatest quotes is, "When the only tool you have is a hammer, you tend to see every problem as a nail."

Different closes are used for different situations, and so you need to know them all. Only when you learn a close by name, will that close become part of your repertoire. Then you need to role-play them; you need to rehearse them. They all work but only if you use them. As we say in recruiting, "I can't guarantee you many things, but I can guarantee you one thing: That Client Company you don't call, you won't make a Placement with." Remember that closes don't always work. They are in your toolbox to amplify your chances of success—a way to 'up' the odds in your favor. As in baseball, the difference between a marginal .250 hitter and a league-leading .350 hitter is only one more hit at every ten times a bat. Great homerun hitters also strike out the most. Great base stealers also get thrown out the most. Etcetera! Knowledge and proper application of the closes can help you to lead your league in production.

Classic Closes

1. Order Blank

This close comes from the real estate industry, automotive industry, and major appliance industry. The salesperson pulls out a form and starts filling it out and as long as you don't stop them, then you are buying. If you try to stop them, they will say that they merely use the form to keep their thoughts organized. Then, when they are finished, they turn the form around to you and ask you to OK it, and they will submit your offer.

In recruiting this would be a Send Out Slip, a Job Order Form, etc. It is best to use this close in person, but this is not always possible since most of us work over the telephone. I have found over the years that an Invoice Worksheet works very well when using this close.

2. Alternate of Choice

This close comes from the egg industry. Apparently in the 1920s and 30s, in the Midwest, there was a malt shop that was selling more eggs than anyone in the country. The head of the egg industry visited the malt shop to find out why. When questioned, the malt shop owner said that he never sold any eggs with his malts until he changed his sales approach and started asking the customers, "Do you want one egg or two in your malt?" The customer would then choose between the options, and the malt shop's egg sales soared.

In our business, this is a way to avoid close-ended questions—those that can be answered by responding "Yes" or "No." Many of you, when presenting your candidates for interviews, use this close. "My candidate is available to speak with you on Monday or Tuesday. Which day is better for you?" You don't ask IF they want to see your candidate. You ask WHEN they want to see your candidate.

3. Puppy Dog

This close comes from the television industry in the 1940s and 50s in New Jersey when color TV was just becoming a reality. Customers would come into the showrooms and look at this new format. One TV outlet that sold more color TVs than any other would have their salespeople say, "You can't really tell what this TV is going to look like until you see it in your own front room or den. Why not take it home and try it out. If you like it, then you can buy it. If you don't, we'll pick it up."

Then, in about a week, the retailer's color TV Tech would show up at the customer's house to see if the reception was still OK. No close on this visit. The retailer said that usually within another week the father figure would come back to the store and ask how much for the darn TV. You see, he couldn't return it now. He would look like the biggest villain of all time in the eyes of his family if he did. Indeed, if you ever have a puppy that you want to get rid of, just ask a friend to watch it for a short time. After your friend names the puppy, they'll never give it back—thus, The Puppy Dog Close.

This is sometimes used when you arrange Creative Send Outs—when you are arranging demonstrations where no real Job Order (JO) exists. You can also use it, in the form of early project work or temp work, to engage your clients and candidates when a long start date is anticipated.

4. Ben Franklin

This is the 'Ben Franklin Balance Sheet Close.' Sometimes it is called 'Baconian Empiricism Through Enumeration' and is actually still in Poor Richard's Almanac. This is apparently how Ben Franklin would make his decision. When faced with the need to make a decision, old Ben would take out a blank sheet of paper and draw a line down the middle. Then he would write down all the reasons for doing something on the left-hand side of the paper and all the reasons for not doing something on the right-hand side. Then he would add up the columns, and the column with the highest number determined his choice.

In recruitment, this is great for either a candidate or a hiring manager who has a lot of information. Their thinking becomes cluttered. By itemizing the info, you help clarify their thinking. Then, you help them with the choices in the column you want them to pick (keeping in mind that they have to say it—not you—in order for it to be true). Once you finish with your column's choices, you refer them to the other column and now you don't help anymore—i.e., shut up! If they can come up with more than just a couple of entries, it will be a miracle. Then you add up both columns and, hopefully, your column wins.

5. Negative Yes

This is sometimes called the 'Is It... Close.' This is for the candidate or hiring manager who is the opposite of the ones we just talked about. These folks give us no information. They are just not sure of what the problem is. Trying to get information out of these people is like attacking an amorphous mass, a cloud. What we are going to do with this close is to attempt to isolate the real objection.

Let's say that we are trying to close a Hiring Manager (HM). This is what we say: "OK, June, but just to clarify my thinking, what is it that bothers you about Jim, is it his education?" You don't hesitate after you say "...what bothers you about Jim?" or the HM might say, "Everything," and you are right back to where you started. Go right into your series of 'is its' without stopping. At this point, the HM will usually answer "No," thus the Negative Yes or 'No Means Yes' close. Then you follow with, "Is it his professional background?" She says, "No." "Is it how he interviewed?" She says "No," etc. So, you see what you are doing. One by one, you are taking away the objections and determining what really is the final objection. Then you can attack that objection.

6. Call Back

The odds are not in your favor when you get this request, but there is a way to handle the call when you do call back. For those of you who know of the principle of 'White Heat,' keep in mind that we are going to attempt to raise the interest level above the 'Buy Line.' This is such a prevalent topic in recruiting that we even have an expression for it. We say, "Time kills all of our deals." That's why calling back after a period of time is not a good thing. When you do call back, you never ask if they have thought about the situation in the intervening time span. If you do, you are going to get the famous 'Yes-No' response—"Yes, I have thought about it; No, I am not interested." Instead you:

a. Introduce a new piece of information;

b. Present a condensed representation;

c. Follow with a new Close.

Only when you do those three things, do you have a chance, remote though it might be, to raise the interest level above the 'Buy Line' and close the deal in your favor.

7. Similar Situation

The 'Similar Situation Close' is sometimes called the 'Story Close' or the 'Back up the Hearse and Let Them Smell the Roses Close.' This one comes from the insurance industry. This is used when the insurance salesman has received the 'I want to think it over' response from his prospects. Before he leaves, he relates a story of a similar situation that happened not too long ago when a couple, not unlike this couple, with a young daughter, not unlike their daughter, wanted to think it over. Then, as the story continues, the original couple was unfortunately killed in a car accident shortly thereafter, and all the insurance salesman can think about is that if he had been a better salesman, the couple's little girl would have been provided with insurance money for the rest of her life instead of being left a penniless orphan. There is a little more to this close than that, but you probably get the idea.

In recruitment, those of you who have some tenure have plenty of similar situations to tell both your candidates and your HMs regarding waiting too long to make a decision and then having the original offer/candidate disappear. Just make sure that the stories are relatable to your target audience.

8. Lost Sale

In this close, you act defeated. You seemingly 'give up.' Then, ask a self-effacing question like, "I need your help. What could I have done better to have brought this deal together so that I don't make this same mistake again?" Their response may bring you right back into the situation, and you will at least have uncovered the real objection.

9. Secondary Question

This close is out of real estate, out of car sales. This is sometimes called a 'Major-Minor Close.' The salesperson says, "The car is $40,000. I just need your OK on the agreement. Do you want to use your pen or mine?" The choice of pens is the secondary question that closes the major question.

In our industry you might say, "I am assuming that you want John to start at the beginning of the month. Now should John bring another resume with him at that point or just come as he did today?" The answer to bringing the resume closes that they want John to start.

10. Sharp Angle – 'Porcupine'

If someone threw a porcupine at you, you would throw it back at them. Or, if something was shot at you, you would shoot it back at a sharp angle. This close is one of my favorites.

You have been trained all your life that if you know the answer to a question that you should answer the question. You have become a little giver of information. The problem is, in recruitment, you don't get anywhere by answering question after question like you did in school.

What happens often in recruitment is that you tend to answer all the questions asked of you by the HM when you are presenting a candidate, only to be ultimately asked to send the resume. Well, that's not what you wanted. You wanted to set up a telephone interview or a face-to-face interview. So, instead of acting like a non-profit information clearing house (which, if you so enjoy, you might look at a career as a reference librarian), I recommend you close on each question asked of you before you answer it. So, for example, the HM asks if your candidate has a college degree. You say, "Well, let me check, but if he does have a college degree, would you like to see him on Monday or would Tuesday be better?" If the HM says neither, then why are you looking to see if your candidate has a college degree? You see, the point is that once the HM asks you a question about your candidate, he has just arranged the interview and you let him off of the hook by only answering the question instead of closing on the question.

11. Tie Downs

There are three types of tie downs: The regular tie down, the inverted tie down, and the tie down tag on. The basic idea with a tie down is that if someone is moving their head up and down in a positive way, it is hard to stop that movement and change to a negative side to side movement.

a. The regular tie down—You say, "Boy, he really does have the experience you are looking for, doesn't he?" 'Doesn't he' is the tie down. "And he would be good for your company, wouldn't he?" 'Wouldn't he' is the tie down.

b. The tie down tag on—They say, "Boy he really does have the experience we are looking for." And you say, "Doesn't he!" 'Doesn't he' is the tag on. They say, "And he really would be a great addition to our company." And you say, "Wouldn't he!" 'Wouldn't he' is the tag on.

c. The inverted tie down—You lead with the tie down. You say, "Doesn't he have the experience you are looking for?" The tie down comes at the beginning. You say, "Wouldn't he be a great addition to your company" Again, the tie down comes at the beginning.

12. What If . . .?

The 'What If... Close' brings non-overlapping situations together. Let's say that you believe that the offer is going to come in at $60,000, and you know that the candidate won't take anything less than $61,000. Well, you have a $1,000 problem. In this situation, we want to focus on 'psyticements' (psychological enticements) such as an expense account, a company car, immediate health benefits (good for candidates with families), early merit reviews, corner offices with windows, etc. We are looking for more ammunition before we fire our 'offer' cannon. For example, we go to our candidate and say, "I was thinking about this last night and what if we go for immediate health benefits (to cover your five kids), and an expense account, but we go in a little bit lower at, let's say, $60,000 to make this package more attractive for the company.

Now, in the long run, by adding those two items you will be making more than the $61,000 you were after. What if we did that?" If the candidate agrees, we go back to the company and negotiate those two items. You see, in most companies (especially larger companies) salaries are not too movable. In many companies they are 'slotted.'

The last thing a company wants to do is to give a new candidate a larger than normal salary so that when it gets out to the other tenured employees (which it will—trust me), a number of them will quit. But 'psyticements' are movable, and we recruiters need to focus more on those and less on salaries (even though a percentage of the salary, or realistic first year's earnings, is how most of us are paid and explains our fixation on that number. It's a shame that we do that).

13. If I, Will You?

The point with this close was brought home to me by Robocruiter, who once told me that he didn't mind cutting fees so much (although he hardly ever did that), it was just that he did mind very much getting nothing in return.

In this case, you say to the HM, "If I cut my fee to 25%, will you give me a decision after each of my candidates is interviewed within 24 hours?" Or, "If I agree to 25%, will you agree to interview everyone I present without a resume since I will be recruiting candidates who are happy, well-appreciated, making good money, and currently working and normally will not have a resume?" In other words, if you give something, you need to get something. It needs to be fair. It needs to be equitable.

14. Reduce to the Ridiculous

This close is for money problems and is based on an amortization table.

Let's take a fee problem. The fee the HM wants to pay is 25% and let's say your candidate makes $60,000, so that is a $15,000 fee. At a normal fee of 30%, the fee is 18,000. So, we have a $3,000 problem. This is what we say to the HM, "You know, Mr. HM, the difference in our fee amounts is $3,000. But let's think of that $3,000 in a little different way. If you take the $3,000 and amortize it over one 'work' year, you get $1.44 per hour. Now, how long do your employees normally stay with you?" The HM says four years. So, you continue, "Four years is pretty much the industry average. Let's take the $1.44 and divide it by four and you get 36¢. Is it worth it to you to not have a candidate of this caliber on board with your company for 36¢?" Hence, the title of the close, 'Reduce to the Ridiculous.'

15. Take-Away

This is used when either side cannot make a decision. With this close, you are going to roll the dice and be very assumptive. You are not going to ask permission to take it away. You are just going to do it. But here is the beauty of this close: You are either going to take it away, so the deal that was not going to go together anyway dies—or you are not going to be allowed to take it away and you will make a Placement. Either way works for you.

You say to the HM, "Listen, I understand your predicament. Usually in our business, if a match is going to happen, the HM is going to say 'Yes' right away, and for some reason you are not. Therefore, my sense is that this is not going to go together. But I tell you what. Why don't we wait until 3 pm? If I don't hear from you by 3 pm today, I am going to call the candidate and tell him that it is just not going to happen. And, if you can make a positive decision by 3 pm, get back to me, and we will put the thing together."

As I said before, you have created a win-win situation. You will either take it away by 3 pm, which means it wasn't going to go together anyway. Or you are not going to be able to take it away, they are going to hire your candidate, and you are going to make a Placement. But let's not let this thing go off into space because it stops you from thinking, it stops you from working, it causes you to be preoccupied 'babying' these things.

So, let's put the HM's feet to the fire. Now keep in mind, they won't necessarily love you when you do these take away closes, but hopefully you didn't get into this business to be loved. You got into this business to make serious money. You get that through making Placements—lots of them. And you get those Placements by getting decisions. The take-away close is one way to get you the decisions you need.

23   THE POWER OF GOAL SETTING

THE PHONE RANG. I ANSWERED. A NEW CLIENT STARTED TO unburden himself. His name was Benjamin. He was concerned about his somewhat anemic production in this sluggish economy. His was not an uncommon call these days. As the year was winding down, many of my clients were looking back over their prior year's production and, if substandard, were begging for help. Ben was one of these. He had heard me speak at a virtual summit and, since I was one of his favorites, was very excited about working with me. He had started his own firm eight years before and had grown to ten recruiters. Now he had seven. His personal production had been as high as $550,000 but was now down in the $300,000 range. Technically, he knew how to do this business, but he had forgotten the 'structure' part of the equation. And so, Ben and I began by building the right foundation. We began with Goal Setting for the current year.

When you contemplate any new venture, you want to make sure that you are not bringing any old baggage with you. You want to approach new goal setting with a blank slate—a tabula rasa. Have you ever been in an upscale restaurant and the waiter brings you a sorbet between courses so that you can cleanse your palette of any previous taste before trying the next course? That's the perspective we want to operate from as we set our new goals for the year. We don't want to repeat the mistakes of the past. We want to leave them in the past. How many times have we heard the famous quote that, "Insanity is doing the same thing over and over again and expecting different results?" Let's not be insane as we plan for the future.

The power of goal setting cannot be understated. A study of Ivy League graduates found that 87% had no specific goals, 10% had goals but hadn't written them down, and a mere 3% had clear, written goals and plans. Ten years later, the researchers followed up and found that the 3% with written goals were earning, on average, ten times as much as the other 97% combined. Crazy, right?

What are the key principles of effective goal setting? I've found that there are four central principles:

1. The goal must be in writing. If it is not in writing, it is a 'wish' not a 'goal.'
2. It must be vividly imagined. Pictures of your goals at your desk are good here.
3. It must be ardently desired. You must really, really want it.
4. You must be committed to it.

If these four principles are in play, then the goal exists, and you will have a good shot at attaining it. At the end of the day, goal setting can be fun. Stay with me. It's easier than you think!

Now, let's take a look at what Ben wanted to personally produce, on his own desk, in the next year. This does not include the production of his recruiters. Once we get his goal number, we can break it down and tell him what he needs to do on a daily basis to reach that number.

Basically, Ben wants to revisit his top production days of a couple of years ago, and so we set a new goal for him of $500,000 for the year.

Remember, you lead best through positive modeling. In one study, recruiters stressed that the help they viewed as the most valuable from their managers was practical, situation-specific advice offered in a positive manner. Always remember that you need to be positive in the implementation of your goals. If you say that you can't do something, your subconscious mind, which makes up 90% of your brain and controls your behavior, will agree with you and you will fail. Therefore, make sure that you are always giving positive signals to your subconscious.

Now, Ben's goals are set for a highly productive year. And hopefully, by following Ben's examples, yours will be as well. If any of this confuses you, be sure to contact me. Let's make this our best year ever. We deserve it, and it is there for the taking!

24 CULTIVATING A GROWTH MINDSET

THE CONCEPT OF BEING THE BEST IN YOUR NICHE OR SPECIALTY is incredibly powerful. It's something that we all intuitively understand—in a free market, the exceptional rises to the top and reaps outsized rewards. This phenomenon is known as 'Zipf's Law,' where the #1 player in a market can generate 10x the results of the #10 player and 100x the results of #100.

But achieving that level of dominance is easier said than done. On paper, the formula is simple: do more of what makes you money and less of what doesn't. But in practice, we often get stuck in our comfort zones, doing things that are familiar and enjoyable but not necessarily productive.

This is where the concept of the 'dip' comes in. The dip is that tough period between beginner's luck and true mastery, where progress seems to stall, and the temptation to quit is strong. But the dip is where the magic happens—it's where competitors drop out and where committed individuals can emerge as scarce and valuable resources in their field.

The key is knowing the difference between a dip and a dead end. Dips are temporary setbacks that can be overcome with persistence and grit. Dead ends, or cul-de-sacs, are situations that will never improve no matter how hard you try. Mistaking a dead end for a dip is one of the costliest errors you can make, because the opportunity cost of investing in the wrong things is astronomical.

That's why strategic quitting is so important. Contrary to the 'never give up' mantra, winners quit all the time—they're just very thoughtful about what they quit and when. Quitting can be a powerful tool for freeing up resources and mental bandwidth to pursue more promising opportunities.

But quitting is hard because our brains are wired for homeostasis. We have a tendency to keep doing what we've always done, even when it's no longer serving us. Just like the dog sitting on a nail, the discomfort has to reach a threshold before we'll take action to change.

This is where habits come in. Your habits—both good and bad—more than anything else, will shape your destiny as a recruiter. The key is to deliberately cultivate positive habits and starve the negative ones. But new habits take time to form, and it's easy to get discouraged when we don't see immediate results. We have to push through what's called the 'plateau of latent potential' and trust that our efforts are not being wasted, but rather stored.

There are specific techniques for building better habits, like focusing on systems over goals, and making the desired behaviors obvious, attractive, easy, and satisfying. But more than anything, it comes down to focusing on the fundamentals with unrelenting discipline.

For recruiters, this means focusing on the vital few activities that actually generate revenue—things like making marketing calls, sourcing and screening candidates, and closing deals. It means realizing that your real value is engaging clients and candidates person-to-person, not hunkering down behind a keyboard. And it means constantly sharpening your skills and your mindset, never getting complacent.

Because here's the hard truth: success in this business comes down to two things, effort and habit. Effort, in terms of putting in the reps and having the grit to push through adversity. And habit, in terms of ritualizing the behaviors that lead to positive outcomes.

The good news is both of these things are 100% within your control. You can't always control the external circumstances, but you can always control your effort and your habits. That's an incredibly empowering realization.

As you contemplate your own recruiting strategy, think about how you can apply blue ocean thinking to your niche. What unmet needs or untapped talent pools can you target? How can you differentiate yourself in ways that make comparison with competitors irrelevant? What can you do to make yourself indispensable to your clients?

The answers won't come easy, but they're worth pursuing. Because in the age of automation and artificial intelligence, the recruiters who will thrive are those who can deliver one-of-a-kind value. And that's exactly what blue ocean strategy is all about.

So, dream big, be bold, and never stop exploring. Your blue ocean awaits.

With that in mind, as you reflect on your own recruiting practice, think about your habits. Which ones are serving you, and which ones are holding you back? What can you do, starting today, to tilt the scales towards the positive?

Remember, extraordinary results are not a matter of chance or circumstance—they're the product of consistently doing the right things with focus and discipline. The path is simple, but not easy. And that's exactly why it's so rewarding.

Keep pushing, keep growing, and keep believing in your potential. The dip is tough, but it's where the transformation happens. And on the other side lies everything you've ever wanted to achieve in this incredible profession. You've got this!

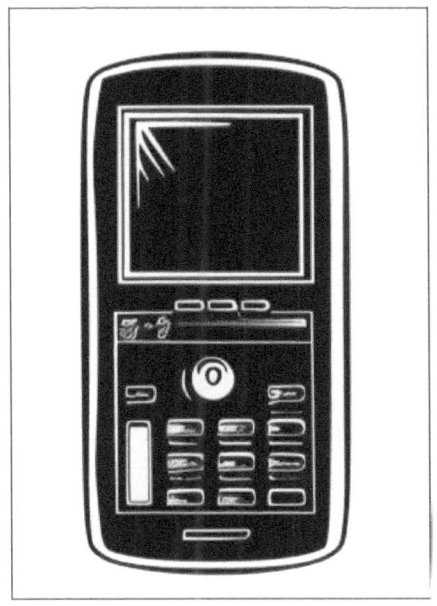

Part 4 | Professional Advancement

"Talent is cheaper than table salt. What separates the talented individual from the successful one is a lot of hard work."

- STEPHEN KING

25 OBJECTION RESPONSES

THE NEW YEAR HAD JUST BEGUN, AND MY PHONE WAS RINGING off the hook. More calls than I can remember receiving in a long time. Good news. The recruitment marketplace is heating up again. The callers are expressing a desire to re-attack their niches. This means they are getting ready to market again—an activity many of my students haven't really concentrated on in months. And with marketing will inevitably come those pesky Hiring Manager (HM) objections, so now it's time to remind everyone how to respond to them.

Why We Make Marketing Calls

But first things first; why do we make marketing calls? We make marketing calls to find companies that fall into three general categories:

1. First and foremost, to find those companies that have a **tremendous urgency** to fill a position. We recruiters are most often paid to circumvent the time factor.

2. Those companies that have a **difficult position to fill**. They have run ads, offered referral bonuses to employees, checked with competitors, consulted with colleagues and extensively interviewed with no success. In this scenario, the recruiter offers these companies a window of opportunity—a 'court of last resort,' if you will.

3. Those companies that wish **to be kept apprised of top-notch talent** as those talented people surface, regardless of whether there is an opening.

It is generally accepted by top producing recruiters that these three types of companies, which we will ultimately place with, make up 4% of our marketplace. Therefore, if our marketplace contains 1500 contacts (which I recommend), then 4% of that marketplace equals 60 companies with which we will place. Multiply those 60 Placements times an average fee of $10,000, and we have a $600,000 per year desk. Multiply those 60 Placements by an average fee of $20,000 and we have our basic $1,200,000 annual operation. That, my friends, is how recruiters, by themselves, bill over $1,000,000 per year. They understand the math.

And now we have been reminded of why we need to make marketing calls. However, when we make them, we are invariably going to hear HM objections, and there will be a tendency to give up way too early.

Objections

Objections are normal consequences of what we do for a living. Unfortunately, many recruiters interpret an objection as a rejection—the HM has decided not to buy—and those recruiters stop selling. Top billers realize that an objection doesn't mean "No," but means instead, "You haven't convinced me yet. You need to give me a more compelling reason to buy"—so top billers don't see the objection as the end to the call, but as the beginning and as an opportunity to win.

The objections we receive can also be 'defense mechanisms' that have been built up over the years because of 'recruiter presentation pollution' that has preceded our marketing call. Think of these poor HMs who have had to listen to defective and shoddy presentations every day of their professional lives. Because of that, they have put up barriers. Then we call, make our scintillating presentation, and get a rude reception seemingly through no fault of our own. We are being asked to pay for the sins of those who have preceded us. It's a shame, but this pollution reaction does exist. Don't let it affect you.

Over time, most HMs have built up an inventory of nos and yesses—many more nos than yesses, as a matter of fact. And when they listen to our initial presentation, we are more likely to get a no just because the HM has more of those to give out. But they do have yesses as well. What the HM is saying with his no is, "You haven't convinced me yet. Your presentation was not compelling. If you give up now, I will know that I was correct in giving you that no. So, go right ahead. I'm still on the phone. Convince me!" Now is the time for us to remember that most sales are closed *after* the initial objections have been expressed.

Stating an objection also allows the HM to avoid making a decision—after all, making a decision is risky business. That's why most people aren't good at it. A 'no' can be just as bad as a 'yes', and most of us tend to avoid either. Just think of yourself the last time you were shopping at the mall and a salesperson asked, "Can I help you with something today?" How did you respond? You probably said something like, "No thanks. I'm just looking." It's a very common response and postpones making a decision.

My final point is this: Since most of what we do is over the telephone, it's easier for the HM to stop us. When we aren't face-to-face with the HMs, we can't read their nonverbal cues—a blush when they make an incorrect statement, fidgeting, tapping their fingers on their desk, etc. Over the phone, they don't have a problem being abrupt with us. But always remember that the beauty of working via the telephone is that we can make many more calls and make many more presentations as we vector in on our 4%. That's a huge advantage if we make use of it.

Questioning Technique

We ask questions to find out where we are in our selling sequence. Those questions need to be open-ended. I always think of the Rudyard Kipling poem when I think of open-ended questions:

I have six honest serving men

They taught me all I knew

I call them What and Where and When

And How and Why and Who

The only reason to make a statement is to prepare the way for asking a question. Never make a statement without following it with a question. The questioner controls the direction of the conversation.

Here are twelve pointers on questioning technique:

1. We ask questions to gain and maintain control.

2. We ask questions to indicate the broad areas the HMs are interested in where we might be of service, and then we ask more questions to isolate the narrow area that is our best opportunity to serve them, and then we ask more questions to pinpoint the exact service we can render.

3. We ask questions to get the minor yesses that will start the stream of minor agreements that will swell into the major river of acceptance of our proposition.

4. We ask questions to arouse and direct emotions towards working with us.

5. We ask questions to isolate objections.

6. We ask questions to answer objections.

7. We ask questions to determine the benefits that the prospect will buy (our services, expertise, and candidates).

8. We ask questions to acknowledge a fact. If we say it, they can doubt it. If they say it, it is true.

9. We ask questions that will confirm that (a) they are going ahead, and (b) we should now go on to the next step in our selling sequence.

10. We ask questions to help our clients and candidates rationalize decisions that they want to make but need a nudge in that direction.

11. We ask questions that close the transaction, whether it's the small closes along the way (such as when to set up the interview) or the final one of start date and salary.

12. We ask questions to solicit their help. People love to be cast in the advisory role. We use this desire to 'help' to our advantage.

When encountering objections, don't use questions that will set up an adversarial relationship between you and the HM. Rather, use questions that will enable you to qualify the objection as real or imagined. Make sure that the real objection has been uncovered. If we are attacking the wrong objection, no matter how compelling our arguments and selling points may be, we will lose.

Generalizations

When we hear generalizations, we can't let them pass unchallenged. We need to drill down and investigate them. We can question them by reflecting those statements back with a question mark on the end. Think of this Precision Model when dealing with generalizations:

They say...

"Too much, too many, too expensive..."

We say...

> "Compared to what?"

They say...

> "People are greedy" (nouns)

We say...

> "Who or what or which specifically?"

They say...

> "Offensive football players should attack the defense (verbs)

We say...

> "How, specifically?"

They say...

> "Should, Shouldn't, Must, Can't"

We say...

> What would happen if...?

> What causes or prevents...?

They say...

> "All Recruiters are self-serving."

We say...

> "All recruiters are self-serving?"

Deal with Objections, and then Move On...

Remember again the 4% rule that governs our success. 96% of the companies out there simply don't need us. They can be nice to us. They can be responsive to us. They can even give us Job Orders and clear our fees, but they lack what we must have. They lack real URGENCY. And so, we need to thank these employers (i.e., 'time wasters'), wish them the best, and move on.

In the immortal words of Thomas Edison, when asked about his seemingly futile quest to invent the light bulb, ..."I have not failed 700 times. I have not failed once. I have succeeded in proving that those 700 ways will not work. When I have eliminated the ways that will not work, I will find the way that will work."

Similarly, when we are making all of these marketing calls, we are doing what Edison was doing. We are finding the companies who don't need our services. In so doing, we are finding the other companies who desperately need us, and those are the ones that will make us rich.

One final piece of advice—this one from my favorite CFO, Ron Allen, who said that we always want to make sure that we are speaking with someone who can say "Yes" and "No"; too often we try to sell to those who can only say "No," and because of that, we get a "No."

Objections come in many shapes and sizes. In my Quick Resource Guide, I enumerate 17 different company objections and responses and four candidate objections and responses.

Here are some of the favorite responses to a couple of common HM objections:

The 'No Openings' Objection

'No Openings' is the big one—the easiest way to get us off the phone.

It's the one we hear with the most regularity. Remember what I mentioned earlier:

"Oh, I guess I didn't make myself clear. I'm a recruiter. I would venture a guess that 90% of the companies I place with don't have openings when I call but do want to be kept apprised of top-notch talent as that talent surfaces. One of the reasons for my call was to see if you wanted to avail yourself and your company of this unusual service.

"What kind of person would you like to hear about should I uncover that person in a subsequent search? Remember, I am a 'contingency' recruiter, so that means that it costs you nothing to speak with my candidates. Only if you make them an offer and they accept and they start to work does my service charge come into play.

"Excellent. I assume no news is good news in that area. To what do you attribute your low turnover?" (Answer) "That sounds great. Of course, we are not solely in the business of filling openings. The majority of the Placements we make and the relationships we have built are based upon a strong ability to locate, qualify, and refer high-performance rarities in our/your niche. We attract and recruit professionals who cost-justify themselves.

"You are fortunate not to be concerned with an opening right now. On a scale of one to ten, one being the weakest link in your company, where do most of the employees fall?" (The HM says a six). "With our recruitment and evaluation process, if I could locate a seven or an eight and keep your payroll cost equal to or lower than your six, would you like to meet that person?"

The 'Too Expensive' Objection

When the cost of our services comes up, try setting the value of the opening versus our service.

Explain to the HM the following basic sales principle: There are three different methods to estimate the worth of an employee to their company: The Multiple of Compensation Method; The Contribution to Profits Method; and The Cost of Replacement Method (and yes, for more information you can Google all three). The following presentation is based on the first method. The verbiage goes something like this:

"Based on studies conducted by the top business graduate schools in the US, an employee's value to their company is usually set at five times their salary. For instance, if your opening calls for a salary of $50K, then the value that person should bring to your company is $250K per year. My service charge, on the other hand, is just 30% of their realistic first year's earnings, which, in this case, is $15K. Or, to look at it another way, my fee is merely 6% of this position's value to your company and that's only for the 1st year! You benefit from the $250K value year after year after year.

My fee is paid only once. When you look at our fee structure in this way, we can definitely bring an advantage to your company. Conversely, taking the value of this position at $250K per year, and realizing that there are 2080 work hours in a year, you are hemorrhaging $120 per hour for each hour that this position remains vacant. Think about it! That's about $1,000 per workday, $5,000 per workweek, etc. Three weeks with this position open will basically equal my fee, and you'll still have that vacancy."

At this point, we can go into selling urgency again—that we are paid to circumvent the time factor, etc.

Universal Response to Most Objections

Here is a universal response that we can use on pretty much every objection that we hear:

"Oh, I'm sorry. I thought you had a sense of urgency and, as you know, we recruiters are paid to circumvent the time factor. When you say (state the objection), really what you are saying is that you don't have any urgency and so don't need my services right now. I completely understand. Should that urgency to fill your vacancy increase over time, please be sure to give me a call. I wish you the best. Goodbye."

Formula for Objections

1. The first time we hear an objection we want to by-pass it—never answer it. "Yes, I can see why you might feel that way. By the way (go on with our presentation)..."

2. If the HM brings it up again, that's when we shut up and listen!!! This may be a condition of working with this client. This may be real.

3. Once we hear them out, we now question the objection. "Just to clarify my thinking, (name), what brought that to your mind at this time?" or "Just to clarify my thinking, (name), what makes that so critical at this moment?"

4. Answer it fully.

5. Confirm the answer. "That clarifies it completely now, doesn't it!"

6. Be diplomatic.

7. Don't ever argue.

8. Don't try to win, try to help.

If we give up when we face initial resistance without giving the HM the information they need to make an informed hiring decision, then both of us lose out. Always remember that the objective is not to overcome all the objections; the objective is to make the Placement.

26 CREATING A MAGNETIC BRAND

OVER THE YEARS, I'VE LEARNED THAT CREATING A MAGNETIC brand is a hidden key to attracting ideal clients and building a thriving recruitment business. It's not just about the services we offer; it's about the essence of who we are and what we stand for. Your firm will develop an image. What it is known for, its reputation, strengths, etc.

Do you want to be known for having the lowest fees? I don't recommend that, but it is a strategy that many firms tend to be known for. I don't want you to be the cheapest. On the contrary, I want you to be at or near the top in fees earned and Placements made. So, how do you become a firm that attracts those new winning projects; how do you become magnetic?

The three essential components of a magnetic brand: positioning, voice, and visual identity. Positioning is all about defining our unique value proposition and communicating it clearly to our target audience. It's about understanding what sets us apart from the competition and leveraging that to create a compelling narrative.

I recall a conversation I had with a fellow recruiter who struggled to differentiate herself in a crowded market. Together, we worked on crafting a positioning statement that highlighted her expertise in a specific niche and her commitment to building long-term relationships with clients.

Much of the change was in how she saw herself, not how others saw her. The transformation was remarkable; she began attracting clients who truly valued her approach and were willing to pay a premium for her services.

Creating a magnetic brand in the recruiting business involves more than just offering stellar services; it's about cultivating an identity that resonates deeply with both clients and candidates. Here are key insights to share with clients running recruitment firms to help them build such a brand:

1. Define Your Unique Value Proposition (UVP): Clearly articulate what sets your firm apart from competitors. This could be your specialized industry focus, your innovative recruiting methods, or your commitment to personalized service. Your UVP should resonate with your target audience's specific needs and challenges.

2. Foster Authentic Relationships: In recruitment, trust and authenticity are currencies. Encourage your clients to build genuine relationships with both candidates and companies. This means being transparent, providing valuable feedback, and prioritizing the long-term success of Placements over short-term gains.

3. Cultivate a Strong Online Presence: A magnetic brand needs to be visible. Advise your clients to invest in a professional website, active social media profiles, and engaging content that showcases their expertise and industry insights. An informative blog, regular updates on LinkedIn, and interactive discussions on industry forums can position them as thought leaders.

4. Deliver Consistent, Quality Experiences: Every interaction with your client's brand should reinforce their reputation for excellence. This includes everything from the initial contact, the recruitment process, to post-Placement follow-up. Encourage them to seek feedback and continuously improve their services based on client and candidate experiences.

5. Engage in Community and Professional Networks: Visibility in industry events, participation in webinars, and active membership in professional organizations can enhance your clients' brand presence. Networking not only builds brand awareness but also establishes your clients as integral parts of their industry communities.

6. Emphasize Your Firm's Culture and Values: Clients and candidates are increasingly drawn to companies whose values align with their own. Encourage your clients to communicate their culture, mission, and ethics clearly in their branding materials and actions. This could include initiatives like community service, sustainable practices, or diversity and inclusion efforts.

7. Leverage Client and Candidate Testimonials: Word-of-mouth remains one of the most powerful marketing tools. Positive testimonials from satisfied clients and candidates can significantly boost your clients' brand appeal. Encourage them to collect and showcase these stories across their marketing channels.

8. Offer Exceptional Candidate Experiences: In the recruiting business, candidates are your brand ambassadors. Ensure your clients understand the importance of treating candidates with respect, providing clear communication, and offering valuable career advice. A positive candidate experience can lead to referrals and repeat business.

9. Innovate and Adapt: The recruitment industry is constantly evolving, with new technologies and changing candidate expectations.

Encourage your clients to stay ahead of the curve by adopting innovative recruiting technologies, leveraging data analytics for better candidate matching, and being adaptable to the changing market dynamics.

10. Measure and Refine: Finally, stress the importance of measuring the impact of their branding efforts. This could include tracking website traffic, engagement rates on social media, candidate and client satisfaction scores, and ultimately, the conversion rates of Placements. Use these metrics to refine and adjust their strategies for continuous improvement. By focusing on these areas, your clients can build a magnetic brand that attracts the right clients and candidates, establishing a strong position in the competitive recruitment landscape.

Next, I turn my attention to brand voice. It's the way we communicate with our audience, the tone and personality we infuse into our messaging. A strong brand voice creates an emotional connection with our clients and helps build trust and loyalty. I think back to the early days of my business when my messaging was inconsistent and lacked authenticity. It wasn't until I found my true voice—a blend of professionalism, empathy, and a touch of humor—that I started to resonate with my ideal clients.

Finally, I consider the importance of visual identity. From our logo and color palette to the imagery we use in our marketing materials, every visual element plays a role in shaping how our brand is perceived. I remember the impact that a well-designed website and cohesive marketing collateral had on my business. It elevated our brand and signaled to potential clients that we were a credible and trustworthy partner.

27 CONVERSATION WITH A SUPERSTAR

Wisdom from 'Robocruiter' and the Total Account Executive, Part Two

THE PHONE RANG. I ANSWERED, AND BOY, WAS I SURPRISED. At the other end of the line was someone I hadn't spoken to in quite a long time and yet someone who had such a dramatic influence on my recruiting life. He was, in my opinion, the best recruiter who has ever lived, bar none. So good at our craft, in fact, that years ago I nicknamed him 'Robocruiter' (half man - half recruiter) after the futuristic movie "Robocop." I introduced him to you earlier. I wanted to give him a nickname so that I could teach his techniques without disclosing his identity. I didn't want him to be bothered by curious recruiters, and I knew that would happen if I divulged his name. After all, we recruiters are not a shy lot.

Robocruiter called because he had committed to a speaking engagement, and since he knows that I do an awful lot of training and standup presentations, wanted to ask me some technical public speaking questions. We talked about speaking, and then our conversation moved into the recruitment training arena. I told him that his concept of The Total Account Executive (AE) was one of my favorite topics. I also said that over the years, I have taught so much of what I learned from him that I couldn't tell where he left off and I began. He thanked me and we went our separate ways.

For those of you who haven't been exposed to Robocruiter before, buckle your seatbelts. I am going to take you on a brief flight through some of his more memorable (to me) recruitment technique snippets. By the end of our journey, you will be able to appreciate his complete mastery of our profession. We will look at:

- The 10 manifestations of failure due to lack of commitment;
- The 8 tenets managers should follow to ensure success in their offices;
- The 6 reasons why we market;
- The 6 qualities of a recruitable Job Order (JO);
- The 5 reasons why recruiters don't close;
- The 13 motivational paths;
- The 5 things you will lose by implementing these techniques!

Sprinkled within these major topics, I will discuss how Robocruiter qualifies his JOs and how he achieves a 100% matching to send out ratio. Whew...I know that's a lot, but luckily for you, I write fast.

So, everyone onboard and let's begin our journey with Robocruiter's definition of "The Total Account Executive."

The Total Account Executive – The Definition

The Total Account Executive is someone who uses every resource available to them - emotionally, mentally, physically, and psychologically - to reach the goal of being a peak performer. This includes, but is not limited to, their attitude, commitment, discipline and intensity at work, knowledge and application of the basics of the industry, planning, follow-through, and willingness to grow and advance in the field. A Total Account Executive sees themself as a professional in this business and carries themself accordingly.

Commitment is Key

In our profession (as in most true professions) commitment is the key. If there is no commitment, then the AE will not feel entitled to ask for, nor receive, the information that they must get from both the Client and the Candidate in order to be successful. And it is our responsibility to our industry to be as successful as we can possibly be. If we don't get that information, we will develop execution deficiencies.

The Recruiter and the Doctor

Let's compare us with a doctor—someone who we all would agree is a total professional. That doctor is committed to helping us gain back our proper health. They are knowledgeable in their industry. We go to the doctor when we have a medical problem, when we have an ache or a pain or we need surgery. We go into the doctor's office and fill out all their forms. Then the nurse takes us to an examining room, and the doctor comes in and asks us all sorts of questions. He gets the facts from us. He goes into great detail. Now, we don't question him. We acknowledge that he controls the procedure. He expects us to give him all the facts. And only when he gets all that information, does he feel comfortable in treating us.

We recruiters are just like that doctor. We have to be committed to excellence in our business just like that doctor. Always keep in mind that our clients' people are the life blood of their company. When they have problems—an opening or a difficult slot to fill—they come to us and ask for our help.

Don't let our Hiring Managers (HM) tell us how to do our business. We are the experts (just like that doctor), and we establish that procedure (just like that doctor).

And just like that doctor, we want open and honest communication with our clients. We would be considered 'quacks' if we took minimal information and then tried to do a serious procedure. The key here is this: we can't be responsible for the results if we don't have control over the procedure.

We must educate our HMs to conduct the recruitment procedure our way because it is in their best interests to do so—and it truly is! If you are going to worry, worry about being respected first—not being liked first. If you are respected, the client will eventually like you...that will come.

The 10 Manifestations of Failure Due to the Lack of Commitment

1. Poor quality Job Orders (JOs) and Recruit Data Sheets (RDSs) – This is when our client company or our candidate refuse to give us the information we need in order to be successful in our Placement activities.

2. Lack of qualifying the interview process to find out when decisions will be made – This starts with knowing when the last day is that the HM can go with the position still open. This is the 'drop dead' date. We then need to know who interviews, when, time between interviews, when the hiring decision will be made, and by whom.

3. Inability to close the Placement – We are afraid to close the deal because we don't have that many deals on our hot sheet. It is professional to close the deal just like the doctor closes the operation.

4. Lack or failure to Market or Recruit consistently – This is a process, not a series of events. We market every day, and we recruit every day. Just as the doctor markets for new patients, we market for new clients.

5. Failure to plan – Professionals plan. Doctors plan. Recruiters plan. None of us 'wing it.'

6. Failure to close on objections – Even with the best of intentions, novelistic things happen along the way. Just as doctors have to be flexible when their surgeries don't go perfectly, so, too, do we need to be flexible in handling objections as they arise.

7. Lack of urgency – We work where there is a sense of urgency. Remember, we are paid, most of the time, to circumvent the time factor.

8. **Lack of discipline** or intensity in completing the assignment – If we don't make a commitment to our business, we won't have the discipline to complete our assignments. They are not always fun, but if they were easy, our clients wouldn't need us. Our business is pretty straightforward, but it can be very intense.

9. **Lack of keeping up to date in the specialt**y – Would you want to go to a doctor for surgery if he was doing surgery like they did it twenty years ago? No, you would not. So why would a client use you if you were not up to date in your specialty, in your niche?

10. B**laming others for lack of production** – This is the 'grass is always greener' syndrome. We must take responsibility for our own actions.

The 8 Tenets Managers Should Follow to Ensure Success in Their Offices

1. Be committed to this business – You can't expect commitment from your AEs if you don't make that commitment yourself. You teach best by becoming the best role model.

2. Be capable of working the basic/practical concepts daily – AEs most respect those managers who work a desk on a daily basis.

3. Provide defined, well-planned goals for your office – Well-defined goals guide the success of an office. You have to know where you are going in order to get there.

4. Provide advanced training for your tenured people – While the 'Classics' never change, the tenured AEs want more—behavioral technique (like NLP) training, advanced negotiating technique training, advanced selling skills training, etc.

5. Provide a fair and rewarding compensation plan – As long as our comp plans are fair and equitable, we won't lose our people.

6. Set up 'minimum standards of employment' – Your weakest link is your minimum acceptable standard in your office. If you expect everyone to bill $250K per year and one AE, who remains employed, bills $150K per year, then $150K is your minimum standard of employment, no matter what you say.

7. Set a positive, enthusiastic, and committed environment – We are in a sales business, and attitude is key for us. Set the tone in your office, and don't let distractions destroy it. If an AE is not feeling well or is upset and exhibiting negative emotions, send them home. Negative people are vexations to our spirit.

8. Be open to talk to AEs about successes and failures – These can be personal as well as professional. Regardless, be open to communication with your AEs.

The Six Reasons Why We Market

1. To develop new and better JOs and client companies – By recycling the companies in our niche, we can find better JOs and client companies and higher level JOs as our trust factor grows.

2. Keeps AEs excited about their industry – When we are consistently marketing, we will upgrade and carve a special place for ourselves within our niche.

3. To become experts in the industry worked – Everyone wants to work with an 'expert'; just have a medical problem and see where you ultimately go—not to your GP, but to a specialist who is up-to-date on the current technology that they will use to treat your infirmity.

4. To get the JO before anybody else does – 'The early bird gets the worm'—be eager and start early. The best JOs are usually the unpublished JOs.

5. To open up other avenues, develop new business – By picking up the phone and speaking into it, you never know what will come your way. New business comes to those who market, in many different forms.

6. To help AEs avoid blanking months – Business begets business. On a daily basis, strive to secure new JOs and new Send Outs (SOs). Those activities, especially the SOs, will lead to Placements.

Marketing With the Feature-Accomplishment-Benefit (FAB)

I am a great believer in making scintillating presentations. In fact, one of my claims to fame is that I was the first person to introduce the FAB concept to Robocruiter. He then took it, molded it, and made it his own and uses it to this day with great success. By implementing the FAB, marketing can be fun!

The FAB presentation is an easy format to learn and can be used with either an 'Idea' presentation or a 'Most Placeable Candidate' (MPC) presentation. It works with either, although I prefer the MPC avenue.

Now, if you use a candidate as an MPC, you can very easily apply this FAB principle. The Feature is what the Candidate does. The Accomplishment is how well he/she did what he/she does—these are usually spelled out in 'concrete' (number) terms. And the Benefit is how those

Accomplishments will benefit a new company—a company to which you are going to take the Candidate. Now you are armed to make a scintillating presentation. You will be able to answer the prospective HM's non-verbalized question ("What can this Candidate do for me?") and you can easily avoid the 'No Openings' box. The FAB presentation also allows you to get excited about the Candidate, and that excitement will be contagious. To reinforce this last point, remember sales training icon Cavett Robert's insightful quote that, "People are more moved by the depth of our conviction, than by the height of your logic." FAB an MPC and you'll see what I mean.

28 RECRUITING THE CANDIDATE

THIS TIME THE PHONE RANG AFTER HOURS. LUCKY FOR ME, I was working late and answered the call. It was from one of my favorite students. She was having problems navigating this sluggish economy. She complained that she hardly ever wrote a 'recruitable' Job Order anymore and that her main problem was once she had a great JO, she was unable to recruit anyone for it. She was stuck!

We talked about recruiting for a while, and it was obvious to me that she had a knowledge deficiency which was leading to an execution deficiency. Yes, she was indeed stuck. The bottom-line was that she had forgotten how to do the "recruiting" part of our business. And so, I began at the beginning...

It Starts with the Job Order (JO)

Robocruiter used to always say that the biggest problem we have in recruiting, other than planning and organization, is working 'Can't Help' JOs as search assignment quality JOs. The 'qualification' part of the jigsaw puzzle was missing.

Those of you who know me know that I am a big proponent of qualifying the JO before we start to recruit on it. The problem is that in this economy, we compound our weak marketing efforts by selecting sub-standard JOs on which to recruit. Then we can't put the thing together, and we complain about the rotten economy when we were merely conducting our business in a rotten way.

Use the Recruitment Column Information

When you are taking The Qualifier JO, and you get to the recruitment column blanks, ask these questions one at a time and in this order*:

1. "Who do you want?"

This question will separate you from all your competition. I am still amazed at how few recruiters ask it. But if the HM missed that you were a recruiter at the beginning of your conversation, he will now realize that you are a headhunter because you have asked for a head to hunt. Usually, the HM will pause while pondering the answer to a question no recruiter has asked them before. But the HM will realize that this is an important question and may want to think about it before he responds. It is normal for them to call you back with many possible leads. "Who do you want?" is a Big Biller question.

2. "Which companies, or which of your competitors, do you respect and want someone from?"

Don't ask "Who are your competitors?" First of all, if you are an expert in your niche, you should already know this. Second, they may not want someone from a competitor. And third, they may want someone from a company not in their field of specialization. Now, don't let them try to put you in a corner by replying that you should know the answer, because, you see, you can never know who they RESPECT and WANT SOMEONE FROM. Only they can know the answer to that question.

3. "Which industry do you want someone from?"

If we get to this question, our JO is going down the drain. It probably means that this HM has not put sufficient thought into his hiring process and this opening.

F-A-B the JO, But Change the A

You need to FAB the JO, much like you FAB the candidate, so that you can make a scintillating presentation. Here is where you remind the HM that you are going to attempt to attract potential candidates who are happy, well-appreciated, making good money, and currently working, and you are going to entice them to move for a better opportunity, i.e., the HM's opening. Thus, you need something to sell, and that is why you need the company information to build a Feature-Advantage-Benefit presentation. What would cause my candidate to leave their job and come to work with your company? What is unique about your company? You must do this in order to place the client company in the most positive light. Remember, your candidate base has to be motivated to consider new career opportunities. The recruiter must constantly be prepared to answer the prospect's often non-verbalized question, "What's in it for me?"—also known by the acronym WIIFM.

Indirect First, Then Direct

I have found over the years that with candidates, most Big Billers prefer to begin with the indirect approach ("Who do you know...?") and then transition to the direct approach ("How about you...? What would interest you in making a move...?"). But you know what? Both approaches work. Use one or the other or both, dependent on your comfort level. It really doesn't matter. Only the results matter.

When you ask who the prospect might know who is qualified, they will invariably answer that they don't know anyone who would be interested in making a move. They simply change your operative word from 'qualified' to 'interested'—that change in words you can't allow and must correct. Tell them that you appreciate them thinking about people who might be interested in making a move, but that you want to speak with those who are qualified. Then you will determine who are the best matches for your JO. Your job is like unwinding a giant ball of string. You will eventually reach the end. You will eventually find the right candidate.

Next, especially if they are interested, they will ask you three questions:

1. "What is the name of the client company?"

2. "Where is it located, geographically speaking?"

3. "What is the salary range?"

These are all 'editing out' questions, and you must avoid answering them. Don't let the prospect make these 'editing out' decisions. You will do that. Here are your answers to those three questions:

1. "This is a confidential search, and I can't give out that information right now. Just trust that it is one of the leading corporations in their niche."

2. "Actually, we have various locations. One is (where the position is located), but we have various locations around the US."

3. "I am so glad you asked me that question. My client wants me to help them determine the range. Based on what I have told you so far, what do you, as one of your niche's experts, feel the range should be?" Then, whatever the prospect answers, you agree with and then ask again, who they know who is qualified and who you can speak to.

And finally, the last question—and it's a biggie:

"Who told you to call me?" Or, "Where did you get my name/number, etc.?"

Here is your answer. It is a two-parter:

"You know, I make so many calls on a daily basis that I frankly don't remember, although I keep everything confidential anyway.

"But I can tell you two things. First of all, it was very complimentary about you, or I wouldn't have tried to reach you. And second, it was no one from your company because I have never called your company before."

They can now breathe realizing that they are not being 'out placed' and that you are not the harbinger of that fate. They will now talk to you.

Bottom-line of the two approaches—Indirect and Direct:

Indirect positives: You get better cooperation, and you get referrals.

Indirect negatives: It is longer, and you can be seen to be 'beating around the bush.'

Direct positives: It is short, and you are saying what you mean.

Direct negatives: The potential recruit will edit out people to recommend to you who might compete with them for the position down the road, and you can create egomaniacs by making the potential recruit feel too special.

CLAMS

Keeping WIIFM in mind, most Big Billers find that candidates will move for one (or more) of five major motivators. These can be remembered by using a second acronym, '**CLAMS.**'" And, interestingly enough, they seem to be important in this ranking order with Challenge being the most important, then Location, etc. Note that Money is the fourth reason why people will move—not the first.

I. Challenge of the new position

- Ask, "What challenges you in your current position?"
- Ask, "Professionally speaking, what would you rather be doing?"
- Ask, "Define for me your 'perfect' position description."
- Ask, "What would you like to do in your new position?"

II. Location of the position

- Ask, "Where did you grow up?"
- Ask, "Where does most of your family live?"
- Ask, "Where would you and your family prefer to live?"
- Ask, "What are your hobbies?"

III. Advancement potential

- Ask, "What is your next step up the ladder?"
- Ask, "What position would you like to have next year at this time?"
- Ask, "What will be the last position you will attain with this company?"
- Ask, "How have you moved up in the company in relation to your peers?"

IV. Money

- Ask, "What is your current salary?"
- Ask, "Is your current salary where you think it should be?"
- Ask, "What salary would it take to move you to another company?"
- Ask, "When was your last raise?"

V. Stability of the company

- Ask, "How stable is your current company?"
- Ask, "Have you had many lay-offs or reductions-in-force?"
- Ask, "Have your reviews and/or raises been put on hold?"
- Ask, "Have your company's plans for the future been altered?"

29 MPCS

Okay, let's talk about the art and science of recruiting the most placeable candidates. Because let's face it, without great talent, even the juiciest Job Order is just a piece of paper.

First things first, though—a little context. Every month, I dive into the latest Bureau of Labor Statistics data to get a pulse on the employment market. And what I've found, time and time again, is that for the skilled professionals we typically place—think college-educated, white-collar roles—unemployment is practically nil. We're talking 3-4% max.

What does that mean for us as recruiters? It means we can't just post and pray. The candidates we need are already working, and they're not actively looking to make a move. If we want to get their attention, we need to sell them on the opportunity.

But before we can do that, we need to make sure we've got a solid Job Order to work with. That's where the 'doctor analogy' comes in. Just like a physician diagnoses a patient's condition before prescribing treatment, we need to thoroughly qualify the Job Order before we start recruiting.

We need to understand not just the basic requirements, but the hiring manager's ideal candidate profile. What companies do they admire? Who are their top competitors? If they could poach anyone in the industry, who would it be? The more specific, the better.

Once we have a clear picture of the 'most placeable candidate,' it's time to craft our pitch. And that's where the FAB formula comes in: Features, Advantages, Benefits.

We start by highlighting the key features of the role and company—the things that make it unique and attractive. Then we translate those features into advantages for the candidate. How will this opportunity help them advance their career, acquire new skills, or make a bigger impact?

Finally, we paint a picture of the benefits—the personal and professional rewards they can expect by making the move. Armed with our compelling pitch, it's time to start sourcing. And here's where opinions differ. Some recruiters prefer to start with an indirect approach, asking for referrals and recommendations. Others like to go straight to the direct ask: "How about you? What would it take to get you to consider a new opportunity?"

Personally, I like to mix it up. I'll usually start with the indirect approach to warm up the conversation and build rapport. But if I sense genuine interest, I'm not afraid to pivot to a more direct line of questioning.

Regardless of your approach, there are a few key things to keep in mind. First, be prepared for objections. Candidates will want to know the name of the company, the location, the salary range—all the things that could be potential deal-breakers. Your job is to keep them focused on the opportunity itself, not the logistics.

Second, remember the CLAMS acronym. The five main reasons people change jobs are Challenge, Location, Advancement, Money, and Stability. Notice again that money is fourth on the list—not first. Too many recruiters lead with comp and wonder why they get shot down. Focus on the other motivators first, and the money will take care of itself.

Finally, don't give up too easily. Recruiting is a marathon, not a sprint. Even if you don't get a bite on the first call, keep the conversation going. Check in after a few days with a new nugget of information and a fresh angle on your initial presentation. Persistence pays off.

I remember one candidate I recruited years ago for a tough-to-fill software architect role. The guy was happy where he was and had no intention of leaving. But I knew he was an ideal fit for my client, so I kept at it.

Every week, I'd send him a new data point about the company's growth, or an article about their cutting-edge tech stack, or a quote from one of their customers raving about the product. Slowly but surely, I could sense his interest growing.

After nearly two months of gentle nurturing, he finally agreed to an exploratory call with the hiring manager. Fast forward a few weeks, and he was signing the offer letter for a 30% pay bump and the chance to build something truly groundbreaking.

That, my friends, is the power of tenacious, targeted, value-driven recruiting. It's not about smooth talk or hard sells—it's about deeply understanding your candidate's needs and desires, and then moving heaven and earth to find the right opportunity to fulfill them.

Go forth and recruit with purpose, with empathy, and with a relentless commitment to the art of the possible. Your clients (and your commission checks) will thank you for it.

30 BRANCHING OUT

DIVERSIFYING YOUR BUSINESS CAN OPEN UP A NEW WORLD OF possibilities and increase income streams and a more consistent cash flow. Let's take a look at the world of working a blended recruitment desk and discover how adding contract staffing to your recruiting repertoire can take your business to the next level.

But before we get into the nitty-gritty, let me tell you a little story. Back in the early days of my recruiting career, I was working at a firm that specialized in direct hire Placements. We were good at what we did, but we were missing out on a huge chunk of the market by not offering contract staffing.

One day, our CEO came back from a conference where he had heard a presentation by Alan Schoenberg, the founder of MRI Network. Alan was a legend in the recruiting world, and he was a big proponent of what he called the 'one-stop supermarket of employment services.' And less noteworthy, he's the person who hired me to come on board with MRI Corporate.

Alan's idea was simple: if we could offer our clients a full range of staffing solutions—from direct hire to contract to contract-to-hire—we could become their go-to resource for all their hiring needs. We could build deeper, more valuable relationships and generate more consistent revenue streams.

It was a lightbulb moment for our CEO, and he came back to the office fired up to implement a blended desk model. At first, many of us were skeptical.

We were comfortable with our direct hire process and didn't want to mess with the complexities of contract staffing. But as we dug into the numbers, the benefits became clear. By adding contract staffing to our mix, we could:

1. Increase our billings and profits
2. Smooth out the feast-or-famine cycle of direct hire Placements
3. Provide a more comprehensive service to our clients
4. Save deals that might otherwise fall through due to hiring freezes or budget constraints
5. Build a sellable asset for the future

Of course, implementing a blended desk wasn't without its challenges. We had to figure out the whole back-office piece—payroll, benefits, workers' comp, etc. But partnering with a reputable contract staffing back-office provider made that part a breeze.

The real key was learning how to sell contract staffing to our clients and candidates. And that's where the rubber really met the road.

On the client side, we had to educate hiring managers on the value of contractors. We talked about how a contract Placement could help them: - Get an immediate resource to stop the bleeding on a critical project – 'Test drive' a candidate before making a permanent hiring decision - Shift headcount costs from fixed to variable - Access specialized skills and expertise on-demand.

We also had to get comfortable talking about the financials in a new way. Instead of just quoting a one-time Placement fee, we had to discuss hourly bill rates, markups, and the true cost of a vacant position in terms of lost productivity and opportunity costs.

On the candidate side, we had to get better at identifying and attracting professionals who were open to contract work.

We looked for: - People between permanent roles who wanted to keep their skills sharp and avoid resume gaps - Seasoned experts who preferred the flexibility and variety of project-based work - Retirees looking to stay engaged in the workforce on a part-time or temporary basis - Folks who had been displaced and needed a foot back in the door.

We also had to educate candidates on the benefits of contracting, such as: - The ability to try out a company or role before making a long-term commitment - The potential to earn a higher hourly rate than in a comparable permanent position - The flexibility to take time off between assignments for travel, family, or personal projects - The opportunity to build a diverse skill set and professional network.

It took some time and effort to get our blended desk humming, but once we did, the results spoke for themselves. We saw a 30% increase in revenue in the first year alone, and our client retention and satisfaction scores soared. But beyond the financial rewards, implementing a blended desk made us better recruiters. It forced us to think more holistically about our clients' needs and challenges. It required us to develop deeper business acumen and consultative selling skills. And it allowed us to build more authentic, value-added relationships with our clients and candidates.

Therefore, if you're on the fence about adding contract staffing to your desk, I encourage you to take the leap. With the right mindset, training, and support, it can be a game-changer for your business and your career. As Alan Schoenberg used to say, "In business, you're either growing or you're dying." So why not choose growth? Embrace the blended desk model and watch your business flourish.

And if you need a little help along the way, just remember the wise words of my old boss: "If you want to go fast, go alone. If you want to go far, go together." Surround yourself with smart, supportive partners, and anything is possible.

31 YOUR BEST INVESTMENT

In the swiftly shifting terrain of today's business world, the role of training has never been more pivotal. The era when simple on-the-job training could carry you through has passed. Now, to carve out a competitive edge, it's essential to dive into deep, comprehensive training and development programs. These are not just enhancements but necessities that equip your team with the latest skills and knowledge, keeping them abreast of industry innovations.

The Training Journey: An Evolution

Training methodologies have evolved significantly, transforming into a rich tapestry of programs designed to meet the nuanced needs of every organization. Whether it's elevating your recruiters' prowess in pinpointing exceptional talent or refining your sales team's negotiation tactics, the right training program is out there, waiting to propel you toward your objectives.

Recruiter Training: The Talent Magnet Strategy

Training for recruiters typically spans two vital areas: identifying and drawing in unparalleled talent and mastering the nuances of interviewing and candidate evaluation. And effectively marketing your services to new clients. The most effective training marries these focuses, cultivating recruiters who are not just proficient but exceptional. LinkedIn's Talent Acquisition Training Program can offer considerable help on the candidate side, offering recruiters the skills to navigate its vast network to spot and assess candidates with precision. Another gem is our own Elite Recruiter Masterclass (elite.recruitmasterclass.com/bigbiller). This robust program is a beacon for those seeking to amplify their recruitment results, ensuring efficiency and excellence are within easy reach.

Be Careful Who You Learn From

The landscape of business coaching and recruitment training has undergone its own revolution. From videos on YouTube and TikTok to webinars from all manner of new age prophets of business success. I take many of these with a grain of salt. Not that they aren't engaging, and they may even have a few good ideas. But what is typically missing is 'The System,' a series of proven steps that will work for anyone who is willing to put forth the effort. A to Z, Soup to Nuts proven formulas and strategies to take you from good to great.

The Unmatched Value of Training

The dividends of investing in training are manifold. Recruiters gain an enhanced capability to network with potential candidates swiftly and effectively, alongside a deeper insight into attracting top-tier talent. Sales advisors, on the other hand, enjoy a sharpened skill set for market penetration, a proficient command of digital engagement tools, and an enriched arsenal for strategic selling and objection handling.

Choosing the Perfect Training Path

Selecting a training program for your team is a journey unto itself. Factors to weigh include your firm's scale, budget, training needs, and preferred learning format. Engage with prospective providers to peel back the layers of their offerings, ensuring alignment with your goals. Seek programs that promise not just skill enhancement but a transformation in how your team approaches sales and recruitment in the digital age. These should offer insights into strategic planning, objection navigation, and cultivating robust client and candidate relationships. If you're poised to elevate your recruitment and sales teams to unprecedented levels of achievement, reach out to me at bob@the-marshallplan.org. Let us give you a tour of our coaching and training offerings and help you discern if we're the right fit for your ambitions. Don't let this chance slip by—embracing training is your gateway to excelling in the dynamic landscape of today's business world.

32   BE BAD TO BE GOOD

I've spent countless hours poring over training materials, absorbing every nugget of wisdom from industry experts. But at some point, I had to step out of the classroom and into the arena. I had to pick up the phone, dial that first number, and face the inevitable rejections head-on.

It's like learning to swim. You can watch all the instructional videos you want, but until you dive into the water and feel the resistance against your limbs, you'll never truly understand what it takes to stay afloat. Or like stepping into a boxing ring. You can study every move, every combo, but until you feel the sting of a punch, you won't know how to roll with the blows.

In sales, it's the same. The script is just words on a page until you breathe life into them. It's not about reciting lines; it's about the way you deliver them. The tone, the inflection, the confidence that comes from having been in the trenches. And that confidence only comes from having stumbled, having fumbled, and having picked yourself up again.

It just basically takes 25 attempts of sucking at something to kind of figure out the flow of how the script works. I can give you the words to say right now, but it's not about the words. Words are 20% of it. Eighty percent of it is how you say the words.

I've watched many teams struggle through those first awkward calls. The stammering, the nervous laughter, the long silences. But with each attempt, they grew stronger. They learned to anticipate objections, to think on their feet, to find the right words in the moment.

And it's not just the sales team that needs this baptism by fire. Every single person in your organization, from the receptionist to the CEO, must be ready to step up to the plate. Because in business, every interaction matters. Every dropped ball is a lost opportunity.

So, we train, we drill, we role-play. We make it clear that sales is everyone's responsibility. And slowly but surely, we're building a well-oiled machine. A team that can handle any curveball, that can close any deal.

It's not easy. It's not comfortable. But it's necessary. Because in the end, there's no substitute for experience. No replacement for the hard-earned wisdom that comes from being in the game, day after day, call after call.

I've always believed in the saying that it takes 10,000 hours to become truly skilled at something. But in the fast-paced world of recruitment, where every minute counts, I've come to realize that it's not just about the hours you put in; it's about the quality of those hours. This second necessary quality element is a 'feedback loop' that allows you to spot errors as they occur and correct them.

Ideally that feedback comes from someone with an expert eye and so every world-class sports champion has a coach. If you practice without such feedback, you don't get to the top ranks. The realization of the importance of a coach is why I joined the ranks of recruitment coaches so many years ago. That, and that I found I was good at it.

Back when I started as a rookie recruiter, I remember fumbling through calls, stumbling over objections, feeling like a fish out of water. But with each call made, each rejection faced, each success celebrated, I could feel myself growing stronger, more confident, more adept at navigating the twists and turns of this challenging profession.

It's not just about putting in the time; it's about what you do with that time. It's about learning from every interaction, honing your skills with every conversation, adapting to every new challenge that comes your way. It's about pushing yourself beyond your comfort zone, pushing through the doubts and fears that hold you back.

As I look back on my journey, I see how far I've come from those early days of uncertainty. The hours spent on the phone, the hours pouring over data and strategies, the hours building relationships and trust with clients and candidates alike—all of them have contributed to my growth and development first as a recruiter and then as a recruitment coach and trainer.

I've learned that becoming skilled at a new job isn't just a matter of clocking in the hours; it's about immersing yourself fully in the role, embracing every opportunity to learn and grow, and staying resilient in the face of setbacks. It's about persistence, dedication, and a relentless pursuit of excellence.

As I continue on this path, I remind myself that it's not about reaching a specific number of hours—it's about the journey itself. It's about the process of transformation, the evolution from novice to expert, the constant striving for improvement. And with each passing day, you're one step closer to mastering this craft, one call at a time.

If you're just starting out, don't be afraid to fail. Embrace it. Learn from it. And know that with each mistake, you're one step closer to mastery.

Part 5 | Mastery & Innovation

"Innovation distinguishes between a leader and a follower."

— STEVE JOBS

33 PLANNING & ORGANIZATION

THIS TIME WHEN THE PHONE RANG, I KNEW WHO WAS CALLING. Benjamin was punctual and anxious to get started. During our last session, Ben and I had covered two of the five points in the Monitoring Star. We had discussed, in detail, Yearly Goals and Quarterly Goals. Now it was time to discuss the final three points of the star: The Daily Planner, Modularization & Blitzing, and the 100 Point Sheet. Once we finished with all five major topics, Ben would possess the necessary structure and monitoring systems so that he would be well on his way to achieving his new year goals.

The Monitoring Star

Ben began with a series of questions. How was he going to complete all of the calls we had determined he needed to make? How was he going to stay on track? How would he remember everything? I stopped him. First things first. At the beginning there is the daily plan.

The Daily Planner

I believe in daily planners because they work. I like the paper format but am fine with the electronic format as well, as long as they are founded on multi-tasking and are modularized.

Multi-Task Foundation

When I say that the planner should be founded on multi-tasking, I mean that I want to encourage my client recruiters to move freely within the call depending on how the call naturally unfolds. I learned long ago that sometimes marketing turns into recruiting and recruiting turns into marketing. And so, my planner is multi-task oriented which enables my client recruiters to take the most out of each call.

At least five possibilities exist on each call: You can Direct Market, Indirect Market, Direct Recruit, Indirect Recruit and Information Gather. This allows you to get something positive out of each call, which in turn encourages you to rush right into your next call. It's all a cascade of successes that further anchors in your subconscious mind that this business is a lot of fun! Not only does this work, but the top recruiters found this out a long time ago, and that's why they make this business look so easy.

As a traveling trainer, I would sit at their desks and take notes. Let me tell you this, top recruiters are masters of multi-tasking. And for them, this business is a whole lot of fun!

Quarterly Format

My planners are based on a three-month period—thirteen (13) weeks. Each planner has one hundred and thirty-two (132) pages, or enough for two pages (four sides) per day for the 64-66 workdays in each quarter. As a coaching client, Ben will receive four (4) planners each year.

I have constructed my planner so that ninety-four (94) calls per day are possible. My recommendation, however, is to pre-plan about 6-10 calls in each 'hour' block to allow yourself free time within each hour to be reactive (call backs, suggestion calls, new ideas, etc.). It is more fun that way—also more creative and more profitable!

Every day at planning time, you will plan for your next day. During this hour (sometimes longer) you will enter into the planner what you will be doing the following day. This function is **CRITICAL** to your success!

Modularization & Blitzing

The planner will allow you to break your day into hour modules and blitz during each of those one-hour blocks of time. Industrial Engineers tell us that human beings work more efficiently when their workloads are broken down into small blocks of time—as little as 15-minute blocks of time. For our purposes, I like one-hour modules, so my planner has eight (8) of those to correspond to a daily eight (8) hour working schedule.

Compared to average billers, top billers have very large marketplaces. It's not unusual for them to make 75 marketing 'connect' calls per day. That is a lot, and because of that, I very rarely teach recruiters to make that many calls. But I do think that a marketplace of 1,500 company contacts is do-able for anyone. With Ben, we delimited a marketplace of 1,500 individual hiring managers to contact on a quarterly basis. That works out to 500 per month; 125 per week; 25 per day; or 12.5 per morning and 12.5 per afternoon. This number was a concern of Ben's. This is where Modularization enters the picture to help us.

Here is a copy of a basic Modularized Day that I gave to Ben:

The Marshall Plan "MODULARIZED DAY" ©

Modularized Day with Seven 'Action' Modules

The 13 Module Day

Sample Modularized Day with Seven "Action" Modules

Time	Module	Activity
7:00 – 8:00		Drive to work, arrive, pour coffee, etc
8:00 – 8:30	I	Morning Meeting
8:30 – 9:00	II	2-3 Friendly Phone Calls that lead to money
9:00 – 10:00	III	12 Calls = 2 Presentations
10:00 – 11:00	IV	12 Calls = 2 Presentations
11:00 – 11:30	V	10 Calls = 1 Presentation
11:30 – Noon	VI	Morning Paperwork/Computer work
Noon – 1:00	VII	Lunch – *Out Of The Office*
1:00 – 2:00	VIII	12 Calls = 2 Presentations
2:00 – 3:00	IX	12 Calls = 2 Presentations
3:00 – 3:30	X	10 Calls = 1 Presentation
3:30 – 4:00	XI	Afternoon Paperwork/Computer work
4:00 – 5:00	XII	Plan for tomorrow
Night Home Calls	XIII	2-3 Planned Calls

1. Rhythm and Production will increase during the four morning (bold) and three afternoon (bold) 'Action' Modules.

2. All 'Presentation Calls' should include multi-tasking (when possible) to increase the success of each Action Call. Five multi-tasking options are possible on each call: Direct Marketing; Indirect Marketing; Direct Recruiting; Indirect Recruiting; and Information Gathering.

3. Don't plan too tightly within each module. Allow for reactive 'slush' time (call backs, last minute preps, handling emergencies, etc.).

4. Once the individual module time has expired, promptly move on to the next module.

Now we had our outline. It would flux with the type of changing activity (searches, preps, debriefs, etc.) that Ben had on his desk, but we wanted to stay, as close as possible, to this framework.

Ben agreed that he could do this on a daily basis. But, since he probably wouldn't make daily Placements, how would he know if he was staying on track, if he was going to be successful?

Monitoring Devices and Call Accounting Systems

Ahhh, the many call accounting systems and the latest software versions thereof. Which one should you choose? Well, I am here to tell you to not choose any of them. And don't tell me about the efficacy of the most recent version of a call accounting system that measures time on the phone.

First of all, they usually monitor only outbound calls, not incoming calls. But that being said, and more importantly, they don't measure 'effectiveness' of the phone call. A bunch of one-minute phone calls don't equal success. In the immortal words of UCLA basketball coach, John Wooden, "Never mistake activity for achievement." And besides that, we want to reach that magical 3-5 minute time window where rapport is established.

There was only one monitoring device for Ben...and that was the classic 100 Point Sheet.

The 100 Point Sheet*

This monitoring device was created by a recruiting firm owner who possessed advanced college degrees in mathematics and computer science and wanted to objectively measure a very subjective business. He wanted to insure that his recruiters would ultimately be successful. He came up with this method that awarded more points for the activities that were 'central' to making a Placement. A marketing attempt was given one point. A marketing presentation was given one point. Matching calls (where a Job Order preexisted) were given three points to either the Hiring Manager or the Candidate. Send Outs were awarded 15 points, etc. This formula has been modified over the years, but the intent is still the same.

Here is the modified 100 Point Sheet that I sent to Ben:

The Marshall Plan "WEEKLY 100 POINT SHEET"

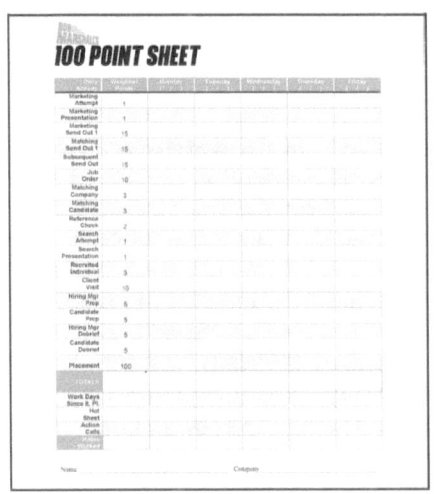

The 100 Point Sheet is designed to show you where you are at any given point during the day. For instance, if it is lunchtime and you have 50 points or more, you are doing well. If, on the other hand, you only have 25 points, then you didn't have a good morning, and you had better kick it up a notch in the afternoon to make up the deficit. The idea is that if you attain over 100 points per day (and your ratios are normal) then you will make Placements. If not, then you won't. Simple as that! One of the obstacles that we all face in this business is that we sometimes get so caught up in the ancillary tasks during our day (long strategy sessions, figuring out who to call next, entering information into our computer databases, chasing the same person all day long, etc.) that we miss the tasks that are central to making a Placement, i.e., Action Calls and Send Outs.

This sheet also allows you to feel rewarded even when you didn't make a Placement (not usually a daily occurrence in recruitment) as long as you reach and/or exceed the century mark. Like any good map, this 100-point sheet forces you to stay on target. I promise you it works! However, it does measure performance, so don't use it if you are afraid to be measured. But without benchmarks, your job becomes more like a game of golf with no scorecard or a game of football with no final score. That's pointless, isn't it? In the words of one of our legendary managers, "Inspect what you expect."

SPECIAL NOTE

The minimum GOAL is to achieve either 100 points or 25 action calls on a daily basis!

Now It's Time for Execution

Now we have in place the plan for each day (The Daily Planner), the structure for each day (Modularization & Blitzing) and the evaluation scheme for that same day (The 100 Point Sheet). Now it's time for Ben to start executing the plan. No knowledge deficiencies now. The tools are in his hands and, by extension, in yours. Remember the words of Goethe, "Whatever you can do, or dream you can, begin it. Boldness has genius and power and magic in it."

34 BLUE OCEAN THINKING

As I hung up the phone after a recent conversation with my client, Ron, I realized that the key to long-term success in this industry is to stand out from the crowd. It's not enough to simply follow the herd and do what everyone else is doing. No, to truly excel in the world of recruiting, one had to be different, to be more than just another face in the crowd. There is a term for this called the 'Blue Ocean Strategy,' based on a great book by W. Chan Kim & Renée Mauborgne.

I thought back to my early days in the business, when I had first discovered the concept that today we would call the Blue Ocean Strategy. It was a revolutionary idea, one that challenged the conventional wisdom of the industry. Instead of competing in the same crowded market as everyone else, the Blue Ocean Strategy encouraged companies to create their own uncontested market space, to make the competition irrelevant.

And that's exactly what I had done in my own career. I had refused to play by the same rules as everyone else, instead forging my own path and creating my own unique value proposition. I had become known as the recruiter who could find the impossible to find candidates, the ones that no one else could track down. I also learned to enter the client companies at a much higher level than everyone else.

It isn't just about being different for the sake of being different. No, to truly succeed in this business, you have to be passionate about what you were doing. You have to believe in the value of your work, in the impact that you are making on people's lives.

Imagine a group of fishermen all vying for the same narrow pool of fish in a crowded, blood-red sea. That's the red ocean—a space defined by fierce competition, commoditized offerings, and shrinking profits. It's a race to the bottom where everyone is fighting over scraps.

Now imagine a brave fisherman who ventures out into uncharted blue waters. He's all alone, but he's also free to fish as he pleases without worrying about competitors. He can experiment with new methods, access untapped schools of fish, and command premium prices for his unique catch. That's the blue ocean—a space where you make the competition irrelevant by creating uncontested market space.

As a recruiter, you face the same choice. You can battle it out in the red ocean of generalist firms, all chasing the same active candidates and competing on price. Or you can sail for the blue ocean by specializing in a niche, developing rare expertise, and delivering unique value that clients can't get anywhere else.

In the red ocean, you're a vendor. In the blue ocean, you're a trusted advisor. In the red ocean, you're selling a commodity. In the blue ocean, you're providing a strategic service. The differences are stark, and they're reflected in everything from your fee structure to your client relationships.

But here's the thing: blue oceans don't stay blue forever. Sooner or later, competitors will take notice and start to invade your space. That's why true Blue Ocean Strategy is about continuous innovation

—consistently staying one step ahead of would-be imitators. It's about routinely asking how you can add more value, solve bigger problems, and deliver better results than anyone else in your market.

Of course, executing the Blue Ocean Strategy is no small feat. It requires a willingness to break from convention, to zag when others zig. It demands a relentless focus on creating value for your clients, not just extracting value for yourself. And it necessitates a long-term orientation, sacrificing short-term wins for sustainable competitive advantage.

But for those who can pull it off, the rewards are immense. Not only do blue ocean firms enjoy higher profits and faster growth, but they also report higher levels of job satisfaction and employee engagement. Because let's face it—it's a lot more fun to pioneer a new market than to slug it out in a crowded one.

I've seen too many recruiters come and go over the years, burnt out and disillusioned by the constant grind of the job. They had lost sight of why they had gotten into the business in the first place, of the joy and satisfaction that came from helping people find their dream jobs.

But for those of us who truly loved what we did, who woke up every morning excited to tackle the challenges of the day, there was no greater feeling in the world. We were the ones who would always find a way to succeed, no matter how tough the market got or how fierce the competition became.

35 THE SUCCESS PYRAMID

The phone rang. It was Craig, a recruitment firm owner from Westwood, California—home of my alma mater, the University of California, Los Angeles (UCLA). I often think of UCLA...

One of the reasons I went to UCLA was that I wanted to be proud when I was asked where I received my college degree. And it worked. I am proud when asked that question. But, in addition to my diploma, I gained something else along the way. I became aware of the teachings of our legendary basketball coach, John Wooden—The Wizard of Westwood. I still remember watching him from the student section at Pauley Pavilion as the Bruins were warming up before a game, his calm professionalism, his rolled-up program, how he looked up into the stands behind the Bruin bench right before the tip-off to find his beloved wife Nellie and give her a wink and a wave.

During my college years, I learned about the Wooden Pyramid of Success that Coach spent fourteen years in developing. It requires a lot for those who follow it, but it is a proven foundation to build upon.

In this chapter, I am going to discuss Coach Wooden's pyramid and how the central blocks and the external casings relate to our world of executive recruitment.

The Pyramid of Success

"***Success*** is peace of mind which is a direct result of self-satisfaction in knowing you did your best to become the best that you are capable of being."—Coach John Wooden

Personal Traits

The Central Blocks of the Pyramid

Here are the blocks and descriptions of each (*in italics*), from left to right and bottom to top, that build the Wooden pyramid. After each block, I will add my comments as to how those blocks relate to our business. As Coach always said, "Success is based on simplicity."

Tier One

1. **Industriousness** – *There is no substitute for work. Worthwhile results come from hard work and careful planning.*

Planning is critical to our success. Plan to work a full day and work that plan. Be where you're at. Accomplish more than the day would normally allow.

2. **Friendship** – *Comes from mutual esteem, respect, and devotion— a sincere liking for all. Like marriage, it must not be taken for granted but requires a joint effort.*

Work to establish rapport with those with whom we work. On every call, get the other person to like, believe, trust, and understand you. Only when those elements of rapport are established, can fruitful business relationships take place.

3. **Loyalty** – *To yourself and to all those depending upon you. Keep your self-respect.*

Do what is required. Only you can answer to yourself. At the end of the day, be able to look in a mirror and be happy with the reflection that stares back at you.

4. **Cooperation** – *With all levels of your coworkers. Help others and see the other side. Listen if you want to be heard. Be interested in finding the best way, not in having your own way.*

People love to help. So, ask for that help and they will offer it. And be the first to help others—not for any monetary rewards, but because it is right to do it. What goes around comes around.

5. **Enthusiasm** – *Your heart must be in your work. Stimulate others. It brushes off upon those with whom you come in contact. You must truly enjoy what you are doing.*

We are in a great industry! We help our candidates more rapidly improve their status. We help our client companies become more successful quicker. And we earn what we are worth. Where else can all of those elements come together!

Tier Two

6. **Self-Control** – *Practice self-discipline and keep emotions under control—a delicate adjustment between mind and body. Good judgment and common sense are essential.*

One of Coach's favorite quotes was, "Be quick, but don't hurry!" And always be in balance. We always want to be under control but be fast. Understand the basics of our business, and then use those basics in a methodical manner. The race is won by the steady and quick performer. Avoid the peaks and the valleys by practicing this self-discipline tempered by sound judgment and managed speed.

7. **Alertness** – *Be observing constantly. Be quick to spot a weakness and correct it or use it as the case may warrant. Stay open-minded. Be eager to learn and improve.*

At the end of each day, review your performance and make changes where necessary. Track your numbers and be aware of your ratios. As with all Big Billers, be open to trying new ideas.

8. **Initiative** – *Cultivate the ability to make decisions and think alone—desire to excel. Do not be afraid of failure but learn from it.*

We are in a marketplace where we place with only 4% of our clients. That means that 96% don't need us at any particular point in time. Realize this ratio and let it work for you. One top biller says that 99.5% of everything he does "fails," so that if he can improve his success rate by ½ of 1%, he can double his income.

9. **Intentness** – *Ability to resist temptation and stay with your course. Concentrate on your objective and be determined to reach your goal. Set a realistic goal. Concentrate on its achievement by resisting all temptations and being determined and persistent.*

Stay focused. Try to stay with your plan but adapt when necessary. Use a coach to remind you of the course you have set. The biggest billers develop their niches and then stay within those delimited boundaries. Be dogged in your determination to succeed.

Tier Three

10. **Condition** – *Mental - Moral - Physical. Rest, exercise, and diet must be considered. Moderation must be practiced. Dissipation must be eliminated.*

Vince Lombardi said that fatigue makes cowards of us all. Take care of yourself. Don't abuse your body which is inextricably connected to your brain. When you feel great, that emotion is transmitted to your clients and candidates. Remember, people can't resist an emotion—whether it be good or bad.

11. **Skill** – *A knowledge of and the ability to properly and quickly execute the fundamentals. Be prepared and cover every little detail.*

Become a student of our business. Learn the basics—the classics of recruitment—and use them. When you overcome your knowledge deficiencies, you'll only have your execution deficiencies with which to contend.

12. **Team Spirit** – *A genuine consideration for others—an eagerness to sacrifice personal interests of glory for the welfare of all. The team comes first.*

Think of what will benefit your client and your candidate. Put yourself third. To borrow some of the words of Emerson, once you do this, riches will beat a path to your door.

Tier Four

13. **Poise** – *Just being yourself. Being at ease in any situation. Never fighting yourself.*

One of the great qualities of our profession is that it can be conducted profitably in so many different ways. In fact, when we see trainers fail, it is because that—having learned this business one way—they think that is the only way that it works. Then they compound this mistake by trying to mold their students around the training instead of molding the training around their students.

Learn the basics of our business, and then be yourself and you will attract those who like you just the way you are. To paraphrase Leo Buscaglia, if you are in an 'apple' world and you are a 'banana,' don't try to be an 'apple.' Just be the best 'banana' that you can be, and you will attract 'banana' lovers. And then you will be the happiest recruiter in the world!

14. **Confidence** – *Respect without fear. Confident not cocky. May come from faith in yourself in knowing that you are prepared. And keeping all things in proper perspective.*

There are three sources of confidence: Product Knowledge—knowing your niche; People Knowledge—locating superstars and heroes for your client companies; and Recruiting/Selling Skills Knowledge—learning the classic techniques developed over the years by our superstars. Possess these three 'Knowledges' and you will exude confidence. For more information on this topic see (TFL, February 2011, "The Phone Rang...How to Acquire the Right Attitude," pp. 16-19).

Tier Five – The Top Tier

15. **Competitive Greatness** – *When the going gets tough, the tough get going. Be at your best when your best is needed. Enjoy a difficult challenge. Real love for a hard battle.*

Love to compete. Challenge yourself to be better than you were yesterday. Learn from your mistakes and constantly move ahead. Have fun in this recruitment business—a business that allows you to have fun while making a ton of money. And always remember that if finding strong candidates for our client companies was easy, no one would need us. It should be hard. It should be a challenge. But when we succeed, it is all the more satisfying. To paraphrase John Kennedy, we Americans do things, not because they are easy, but because they are hard.

Personal Traits

The (external) Casing Stones of the Wooden Pyramid

1. **Ambition** – *Properly focused; for noble goals.*

Be ambitious for the right reasons. Ambition is good if focused on the higher good.

2. **Sincerity** – *Makes and keeps friends.*

Like people and use things—not the other way around. Most of us can unmask a 'fake' very quickly and tend to steer clear of those types of people. You need to like people because people are likeable—not for any other reason. Be real and develop real business friendships.

3. **Adaptability** – *To any situation.*

As Charles Darwin said, "It is not the strongest of the species that survives, nor the most intelligent, but the one most responsive to change." Be noted for your flexibility! For more information on this topic see (TFL, February 2010, "2010...The Year to Continue 'Adaptability,'" pp. 1-5).

4. **Honesty** – *In all ways; in thought and action.*

Everyone has heard the story of Diogenes, who went around the sunlit streets of Athens, lantern in hand, looking for an honest man. People still seek that honesty today. It is an admirable quality in any line of business.

5. **Resourcefulness** – *Proper judgment.*

Choose your clients and candidates carefully. Use correct judgment and be jealous with your time.

6. **Reliability** – *Others depend upon you.*

Teach punctuality by keeping your appointments and making phone calls on time. Be the recruiter others can rely on. Give both good news and bad news in a timely fashion.

7. **Fight** – *Determined effort and hustle.*

Tenacity in the battle usually wins the battle. Don't give up. Don't ever give up.

8. **Integrity** – *Purity of intention; speaks for itself.*

Good things happen to good people. If your intention is right, others will be attracted to you.

9. **Faith** – *Through prayer.*

Realize that we are all guided by a Higher Power—however you envision that Higher Power. This force is stronger than any of us and a great source of power to which we can hand over situations that are out of our control.

10. **Patience** – *Good things take time.*

Rome wasn't built in a day. Define your marketplace and get into it daily. Recycle your client contacts on a quarterly basis. It does take time, but with time and 'correct' tenure, you will become more and more successful. After ten years, for example, you want to have accumulated ten years of experience, not one year ten times.

In Conclusion

I hope you liked this quick, abbreviated version of my 'take' on Coach Wooden's Success Pyramid. I am hopeful that you can use this knowledge on your desk to help you to become more successful. As Coach Wooden said, "There is nothing more satisfying for a teacher than watching his students make his lessons their own."

36 FOCUS

I MET RON IN THE EARLY 1990S WHEN HE WAS PART OF A TEAM recruiting me to relocate from San Diego to Atlanta. I liked him immediately. He was very likeable. Ron Allen was a Salesman trapped in the body of an Accountant. Ron had been a CPA for some 30 years. He graduated from Georgia State University in downtown Atlanta and started his business life first with the large accounting firms and then as a Business Broker. Sometime later, for eight years, he was the CFO of a quickly expanding Atlanta Temp firm that grew from $8,000,000 to $165,000,000 during his tenure. In the 1991/1992 period, he moved over to a recruitment company where he had been on the Board of Advisors for the previous seven years. I joined this firm as their trainer in 1993. This is when I had a chance to get to know this dynamo of a CFO.

When we had our regular recruiter class graduations, Ron would be invited in to give the new recruiters his parting words of wisdom before sending them off to their individual offices. I teasingly entitled these talks "By the Numbers" since he was the top financial person in the company even though he rarely spoke about the numbers.

Instead, he focused on giving fatherly guidance—basic rules to live by as a recruiter. Let's go back to those days and see how many I remember. Pretend you just graduated from rookie recruiter training. I get up in front of you and say, "Ladies and Gentlemen, let me introduce to you our CFO, Ron Allen..."

Recruiter Guidance

1. **Don't let anyone talk you into failing.** Don't be surprised if the top recruiter in your new office walks by your desk on your first day and tells you that you don't need all of the recruitment tools that were given to you during your rookie training (daily planners, quick resource guides, scripts, etc.) to be successful. These top recruiters will boast that they don't use those tools and don't need them either. But don't listen to them. Use the tools that you were given during your training classes to become successful. Then, after time, when the tools become a part of you and you reach the level that Abraham Maslow called "Unconsciously Competent," your use of those tools will not be as apparent because by then, you will conduct your business naturally. But always keep those tools handy so that you can easily access them during inevitable slump periods.

2. **This business is an activity business, and it is not an easy business.** This is a pretty straightforward business, but it is also hard work. Never confuse a lot of activity for production. A lot of one-minute phone calls will lead you nowhere. The activity has to make sense, but there has to be activity, nevertheless. You will never make a Placement with a company that you never call.

3. **This business is a Process, not a series of Transactions.** It's important to do everything every day. When you conduct your business this way, you will always have something to do, something to work on. If you start treating this business as a transaction, then, once the transaction is over, you will have to start all over again. If that happens, this business will be rife with fits and starts and

become a very confusing and difficult endeavor. So, treat your business as a process for smooth and constant production.

4. **Don't let money be the end-product**. Money is a by-product of the business you conduct. Your business is finding a suitable candidate for your Hiring Managers, and it is finding a suitable position for your candidates. You do that, and the money will come. In this business, if you focus on the money as the end-product, you will soon be out of business.

5. **When you call in to your client companies, don't talk to people who cannot say "Yes."** In every company, everybody can say "No," but few can say "Yes." Make sure on your client calls that you reach the people, and speak with the people, who can say "Yes." If you only speak to those who can only say "No," two bad things will happen. First of all, you will get nowhere. And second, no one will ever know that you called in the first place. The problem is, from an ego point of view, the people who can only say "No" don't tell you that. They don't say that they can't say "Yes." They just say "No."

6. **We can't be successful as a group unless each one of you is successful individually**. That means learn the systems, pick up the phone, and do the activity. If you have questions, ask for help. Don't muddle through when you are not sure what to do. Ask. Synergistically we can be more creative and bring more to the bottom-line than any one of us can accomplish singly.

The Best and Biggest Piece of Advice

And then came what I always considered Ron's best piece of advice. He said that we are in an 80:20 business—that indeed life was an 80:20 proposition. He would suggest to the new recruiters that they tell their Hiring Managers that if the candidate presented was 80% right for the position, jump all over him and consider yourself the luckiest HM on the face of the planet because no match will ever be a

100% match. And to the candidate he recommended saying that if the position you are interviewing for is 80% right, jump all over it because no position is ever going to be perfect. If it is 80% of what you are after, accept immediately and run to tell all your family and friends just how lucky you have become. Remember, as in life, 100% matches—the so-called 'perfect matches'—do not exist. If you look for them in your JOs and candidates, you will constantly be frustrated, and if you look for them in life, your life will be a tortuous and unfulfilling journey.

The True Southern Gentleman

Ron always had a quick wit and a wry smile. He called pick-ups 'Pick'em-up Trucks' and in elevators he would 'mash' the buttons. Once in downtown Atlanta, when we boarded an outside glass elevator to start our 73 story ride up the tallest hotel in the Western hemisphere, I mentioned that I didn't like heights. In his quick way, he said, "Well, Bob, then look at the door." He loved to play up his Southern drawl and 'perceived' slow Southern mannerisms to get the upper hand on those 'damn Yankees.' He reveled in that. Ron was truly a Southern Gentleman. Like Julia Roberts, he was from Smyrna—a real 'Smyr-fette.' Professionally, Ron had many gifts. He was a special man and touched many, many lives.

37 YOUR IDEAL CLIENT

Some years ago, I had the opportunity to visit the Idaho location of a man whom I consider the best, most complete recruiter in the world. To protect his identity, I will simply refer to him by his first name, Dan. He was part man, part machine, and all recruiter. He was Robocruiter!'

As we covered previously, the seven points he expects clients to agree to is very intensive.

I said, "I can't believe that the Hiring Managers agree with all of your demands."

"Bob, you're missing the point. I want them to disagree with me. You see, I know that most of the JOs I write will fall into the 'Can't Help' category. I say what I say to edit those out. If an HM says they can't work my way, I thank them, hang up the phone, look to the heavens and thank my lucky stars that I found out on 'day one' that this was a 'Can't Help' JO and not 'day fifteen' after I had spent my straight commission time on surfacing multiple qualified recruits, thereby sacrificing marketing time, only to find out that this HM had no intention of hiring in the first place."

I remember that conversation clearly. And what I learned on that cold and snowy morning in Boise, Idaho about how to pre-qualify Job Orders from the best. And that was Robocruiter in action!

38 BECOME INVALUABLE

Let's dive into a topic that's more important than ever in today's digital age: being an accessible recruiter, even when you're not physically present. Make sure your clients and candidates remember you, recommend you, and come to you when they have a need.

The Changing Landscape of Recruiting

Gone are the days when recruiting was all about face-to-face meetings and firm handshakes. With the rise of technology, we can now connect with candidates from anywhere in the world, at any time. But just because we 'can' recruit virtually doesn't mean we should forget the importance of being accessible.

You see, recruiting is a two-way street. It's not just about finding the ideal candidate for your company—it's also an opportunity for the candidate to get to know you and what you bring to the table. And that's where accessibility comes in.

The Power of Presence

Being accessible means being available when candidates want to connect, whether that's through phone, email, social media, or carrier pigeon (okay, maybe not that last one). It means being responsive, keeping the lines of communication open, and showing candidates that they're a top priority.

Think about it this way: if a candidate reaches out with a question, and you take days to respond (or worse, never respond at all), what message does that send? It tells them that they're not important, that your company doesn't value communication, and that maybe this isn't the right fit after all.

On the other hand, when you're quick to respond, attentive to their needs, and always willing to lend an ear, you're building a strong foundation of trust and respect. And that, my friends, is how you attract top talent.

And don't forget to emphasize results. Candidates and Employers don't care about your process—they care about what you can do for them. Share success stories, case studies, and testimonials that showcase the real-world impact you've had on candidates' careers.

Becoming an Industry Expert

But being accessible isn't just about being responsive—it's also about being knowledgeable. Candidates want to work with recruiters who understand their industry, who can speak their language, and who can provide valuable insights and advice.

How do you become an industry expert? It starts with immersing yourself in your niche. Read industry publications, attend conferences and webinars, follow thought leaders on social media, and never stop learning.

But don't just consume information—share it, too! Write blog posts, post updates on LinkedIn, host Q&A sessions on Twitter. Show hiring managers and candidates that you're not just a recruiter, but a valuable resource and thought leader in your field.

Strategies for Remote Accessibility

Of course, being accessible and knowledgeable is one thing when you're meeting candidates in person—but what about when you're working remotely? Here are a few strategies to keep in mind:

1. Embrace technology to extend your reach: From video conferencing to instant messaging, there are countless tools that can help you stay connected with candidates, no matter where you are. Consider Drip marketing for automated personalized and timed emails on a regular basis.

2. Set clear expectations: Let candidates know when and how they can reach you and be sure to follow through on your promises.

3. Be human: Just because you're communicating through a screen doesn't mean you can't be personable. Use humor, show empathy, and let your personality shine through.

4. Stay organized: When you're juggling multiple candidates and conversations, it's easy for things to slip through the cracks. Use a CRM or other organizational tools to stay on top of your communications and never let a candidate fall by the wayside.

They're Paying You to Care, So Care

As I reflect on the lessons I've learned throughout my years in the recruiting industry, one fundamental truth stands out: our clients and candidates are paying us to care, and it's our duty to do just that.

In today's digital age, information is at everyone's fingertips. A quick Google search can yield countless resources on job searching, resume building, and interview techniques. But that's not what sets us apart as recruiters. Our true value lies in our ability to provide the one thing that technology can't: genuine, human connection and accountability.

When a candidate comes to us, they're not just looking for a job – they're looking for a partner, someone who will be there to guide them through the often-daunting process of finding their dream career. They need someone who will check in on their progress, offer words of encouragement when the going gets tough, and celebrate their successes along the way.

And the same goes for our clients. They're not just looking for a warm body to fill a position—they're looking for a strategic partner who will take the time to understand their unique needs, culture, and goals. They need someone who will be there to answer their questions, provide expert advice, and go above and beyond to find the perfect fit for their team.

That's where we come in. As recruiters, it's our job to be that partner, that trusted advisor, that caring ear. We need to show our clients and candidates that we're invested in their success, that we're here to help them navigate the ups and downs of the hiring process, and that we'll be there to support them every step of the way.

But our job doesn't end when the offer is signed, or the candidate starts their new role. In fact, that's just the beginning. We need to continue to nurture those relationships, to check in regularly, to offer ongoing support and guidance. Because at the end of the day, our success is directly tied to the success of our clients and candidates.

Let's never forget the true value we bring to the table. Let's continue to show up, to care deeply, and to be the partner that our clients and candidates need. Because when we do, everyone wins.

The Bottom Line

At the end of the day, being an accessible recruiter is all about one thing: putting candidates first. It's about being there when they need you, providing value at every turn, and building relationships that last long after the hiring process is over. So, whether you're recruiting in person or from behind a screen, remember—your presence matters. Be accessible, be knowledgeable, be human, and watch as top talent flocks to your door.

39 BE A MASTER CLOSER

My colleague and friend John was a remarkable individual who left an indelible mark on me and the recruiting industry. Despite his education in electrical engineering, John possessed an innate talent for sales and recruiting, which propelled him to success in every role he undertook.

His journey in the industry closely mirrored that of this author, as we both started as Account Executives in 1980, transitioned into training roles, and eventually became office managers.

One of the most valuable aspects of being a trainer in the recruiting industry is the opportunity to learn from top performers. John Lewis capitalized on this, gleaning insights from superstar recruiters and sharing them with others, including myself. Two of the most impactful closing techniques John passed along were methods for training candidates to take control of their own closing during face-to-face interviews.

The first technique involves the candidate asking the Hiring Manager (HM) about the interview process and the possibility of concluding their business that same day if everything goes well. By posing this question at the <u>beginning</u> of the interview, the candidate catches the HM off-guard, eliciting a candid response that sets the stage for a smooth closing later on.

The second technique is employed at the end of the interview when the HM typically asks if the candidate has any final questions. The candidate responds with an assumptive close, focusing on how they can help the company and relieve the HM's immediate workload upon starting the job. This approach is powerful because it demonstrates the candidate's proactive nature and genuine interest in contributing to the organization's success.

I remember one candidate I worked with who used this close during his interview. I will call him Dan. After the interview, Dan called me and thanked me for giving him the verbiage for this close. He said that during his individual interviews with the top four people in the company, he used the closing question on each person. He said that each stopped to ponder his question before answering.

He felt that they knew it was a serious question and were not going to belittle it with a 'pat' answer. Instead, they thought about it and then told Dan, from their perspectives, what was most important. Dan said that by gleaning the answers from each of the major decision makers in the company, he now knew how to satisfy each. He was made the offer, accepted, and has had a successful career with this firm.

Moreover, the impact of these closing techniques extends beyond individual job offers. Hiring managers have been so impressed by candidates who ask how they can help the company that they have gone out of their way to recommend other companies for the recruiter to contact on the candidate's behalf, even when the initial match wasn't suitable.

John Lewis's wit, humor, and deep understanding of the recruiting business left a lasting impact on those who have had the privilege of working with him. His willingness to learn from others and share his knowledge has undoubtedly contributed to the success of countless recruiters and job seekers alike.

As I reflect on John's legacy, I'm reminded of the importance of continuous learning, collaboration, and the power of effective communication in the recruiting process. By employing the closing techniques he shared and embracing his approach to personal and professional growth, we can all strive to make a positive impact on the lives of those we serve in this dynamic and rewarding industry.

40 MESSAGES THAT GET RESULTS

Alright, let's talk about one of the most essential skills in your recruiting toolkit: effective messaging. Because let's face it, you can be the best sourcer, the most skilled interviewer, and the most charismatic recruiter in the world, but if your messages fall flat, you're not going to get very far.

The Importance of Phone Communication

Now, I've been in this industry for over 44 years, and one thing I've always been a big believer in is the power of the phone. There's just something about that personal connection, the ability to build rapport and trust, that you can't quite replicate with an email or a text.

But, I get it. We're in the digital age, and sometimes, you just can't get through to your target on the phone. That's where voicemails and emails come in. And that's what we're going to focus on—crafting messages that don't just avoid the dreaded black hole of no response but actually compel your recipient to take action.

Message Basics: The Science of Persuasion

So, what's the secret sauce? Well, it all comes down to understanding a few key principles of psychology and persuasion. Things like:

1. The personal connection: People want to work with people they like and relate to.

2. Peer pressure and social leverage: We take cues from others in our circle.

3. The power of 'because': Providing a reason, even a simple one, can boost compliance.

4. Humor and the 'frog effect': Making someone smile can break down objections.

5. The magic of numbers: From using digits in subject lines to harnessing the power of three.

By weaving these elements into your messages, you can create a sense of familiarity, build credibility, and make your requests feel more compelling.

The Messaging Formula: Your Blueprint for Success

But knowing the principles is one thing—putting them into practice is another. That's why I've developed a simple, seven-part messaging formula that you can use as a blueprint for all your outreach:

1. Recipient's name
2. Short intro
3. Personal connection
4. FAB (Feature, Advantage, Benefit) content
5. Power of competition and fear of loss
6. Call to action (I have arranged...) with a three-part alternative choice close
7. Lost sale close

By following this formula, you can ensure that every message you send is purposeful, compelling, and designed to elicit a response.

Putting It All Together: Scripts and Templates

Of course, theory is great, but I know what you really want—practical examples you can start using right away. That's why I provide my students sample scripts for both marketing and recruiting scenarios. They use them as a starting point, but they must remember—the key is to make them your own. Infuse your personality, your unique value proposition, and your deep understanding of your niche into every message.

The 10 Commandments of Ineffective Messaging

Before we wrap up, I want to leave you with a few things to avoid—the cardinal sins of messaging, if you will:

1. Being too long-winded
2. Being too formulaic or automated
3. Being too dense or difficult to read
4. Being too self-centered
5. Being too vague
6. Being too timid or apologetic
7. Being too formal or jargon-heavy
8. Coming on too strong too soon
9. Being irrelevant to your audience
10. Making typos or grammatical errors

By steering clear of these pitfalls and focusing on crafting messages that are concise, compelling, and customer-centric, you'll be well on your way to inbox domination and recruiting success.

There can be awesome power in effective messaging. Remember, in business your words are often the first and only impression you get to make. Make them count. Craft your messages with purpose, with personality, and with a deep understanding of what makes your recipients tick. Be concise, be compelling, and above all, be human. Because at the end of the day, people do business with people they know, like, and trust. And it all starts with your words. Now, go forth and make every message matter!

Part 6 | Scaling Your Business

"The greatest danger in times of turbulence is not the turbulence - it is to act with yesterday's logic." - PETER DRUCKER

41 GET PAID

ALRIGHT, LET'S TALK ABOUT THE ALL-IMPORTANT TOPIC OF recruiter fees. As you know, this has been a source of debate and confusion in our industry for years. But I'm here to offer some clarity and reinforcement on the matter.

Your pricing represents your value. It's not just about making money—it's about setting the tone for your entire business relationship. When you're the cheapest option on the market, you attract a certain type of client. They're the ones who are always looking for a deal, always trying to negotiate you down, always questioning your value. And let me tell you, those clients are rarely worth the hassle.

I made a decision early on in my career to never be the cheapest. In fact, I'm constantly evaluating my client list and churning out the lowest profit ones. It might seem counterintuitive, but trust me—the clients who pay the least are often the ones who demand the most. They'll drain your time, your energy, and your resources, and at the end of the day, you'll have little to show for it.

Instead, I base my charges on the value I bring to the relationship. I take a deep dive into my client's business, understand their pain points, and identify where I can make the biggest impact. Then, I price my services accordingly. It's not about the hours I'll invest—it's about the results I'll deliver.

And that's where the art of pricing comes in. You see, the key to setting your fees is understanding the degree of pain your client is experiencing. The more acute their problem, the more they'll be willing to pay for a solution. It's not about taking advantage of their vulnerability—it's about recognizing the value you bring to the table.

When I'm working with a new client, I take the time to really listen to their challenges. I ask probing questions, I dig deep into their business, and I uncover the root causes of their pain points. And then, when I present my solution, I paint a vivid picture of what their life could look like without this pain. I help them envision a future where their problems are solved, their goals are achieved, and their business is thriving.

That's when the magic happens. When a prospect sees that you truly understand their struggles and that you have a clear path forward, they'll be drawn to your solution like a moth to a flame. They'll recognize the value of your expertise and be willing to invest in your services.

Of course, pricing is never a one-size-fits-all proposition. What works for one client may not work for another. That's why I'm constantly testing and iterating my pricing strategy. I run experiments with different price points, gather feedback from my clients, and stay up-to-date on what's working for others in my niche.

But I don't stop there. I'm always exploring new pricing strategies to ensure I'm capturing the full value of my services. Dynamic pricing, for instance, allows me to adjust my rates based on market demand and the unique needs of each client. Premium pricing models, on the other hand, enable me to offer exclusive, high-touch services to my top-tier clients.

Of course, pricing is only half the battle. You also have to be able to communicate your value effectively. I've learned that it's not enough to simply state your prices—you have to justify them. I take the time to walk my clients through my process, highlighting the unique insights and expertise I bring to the table. I share case studies and testimonials that demonstrate the tangible results I've delivered for other clients. And I'm not afraid to stand firm on my prices—because I know the value I provide is worth every penny.

For a long time, the standard fee for recruiters was around 30% of the candidate's first-year earnings. And you know what? That was the norm for a reason—it worked. It provided a fair and equitable split between the value we brought to the table and the compensation our clients were willing to pay.

Consider this, every position essentially has the same job description —Add Profit. Each Placement you make with a new client should add multiple times their salary in additional profits or cost savings. The minor fee you will collect is a small investment for the employer.

But here's the thing—the world has changed, and our industry has changed with it. Nowadays, the 'one-size-fits-all' approach just doesn't cut it anymore. The market has become more dynamic, and the value we provide as recruiters has become more nuanced.

I've got clients in the contract staffing space, for example, whose clients are willing to pay 100% or more of a first-year earnings. Why? Because the talent they need is simply that valuable. It's a specialized, high-demand skill set that's worth every penny.

On the flip side, I've got other clients who balk at the idea of a 30% fee. They see it as too high, and they're willing to look elsewhere for a better deal. And you know what? I respect that. Because at the end of the day, our market—your market—will set the price.

So, what's the sweet spot? Well, that's the million-dollar question, isn't it? The truth is, as I said, there's no one-size-fits-all answer. It all comes down to the value you bring, the talent you have access to, and the specific needs of your clients.

Before you start cutting your fees, take into consideration everything you put into being able to work that job order. The computers, software, database, ATS, furniture, taxes, insurance, all of your overhead, all of your support staff. The resources you subscribe to, the business travel as well as your fill rate. How many of those jobs never add any income?

My advice? Aim to be in the top third of your market. Don't be the cheapest option out there, but don't price yourself out of the game either. Focus on delivering exceptional results, and let the market determine the appropriate fee.

And remember, it's not just about the percentage—it's about the overall value you provide. Are you offering a comprehensive, end-to-end recruitment solution? Are you bringing deep industry expertise and a vast network of top-tier talent? Those are the kinds of things that can justify a higher fee.

Keep an eye on the market, stay nimble, and don't be afraid to experiment with different pricing models. The key is to find the sweet spot that works for you, your clients, and your bottom line. Because at the end of the day, that's what's going to keep your business thriving and growing.

42 YOUR BUSINESS, YOUR STORY

As I've grown my recruiting business over the years, I've come to realize that storytelling is one of the most powerful tools in my arsenal. It's not just about reciting facts and figures—it's about weaving a compelling narrative that captures the imagination and inspires action.

The power of storytelling is hard-wired into humans. That's why it resonates so deeply within us. Let's start with the biological aspect of it. When you hear a story, something fascinating happens in your brain. Your neural activity increases five-fold. Neuroscientists call this 'neural coupling.' Imagine a bridge being built between the storyteller's brain and yours. That's what happens when you listen to a story.

Another phenomenon is 'mirroring.' When someone tells you about how delicious their lunch was, your sensory cortex lights up as if you were tasting the same food. The same applies when they describe a horrifying incident or an exhilarating adventure. Your brain reacts as though you were living the experience.

And then there's dopamine, that powerful neurotransmitter that gets released when we're either excited or surprised by a story. It sharpens our focus and helps us remember details vividly. If I tell you a list of facts, chances are you'll forget most of them by tomorrow. But if I weave those facts into an engaging narrative, dopamine ensures you'll remember them far longer.

Stories also stimulate the release of oxytocin, the hormone associated with empathy and connection. This explains why we feel a deep bond with characters in a book or movie, and why we're more likely to be persuaded by stories that evoke strong emotions.

And finally, there's our love for patterns. Our brains are hardwired to seek out cause-and-effect relationships in everything around us. Stories cater to this need perfectly, providing a clear sequence of events leading to a satisfying conclusion.

In essence, storytelling is not just an art; it's also a science. It has evolved over thousands of years as an essential part of human communication, helping us connect, empathize, and make sense of the world around us. It's more than just persuasion; it's about building bridges between minds and hearts.

I had one client who was particularly problematic. They were a no-nonsense, bottom-line kind of company, and they didn't see the point in 'fluff' like narratives and anecdotes. I had a candidate who matched perfectly for a design lead position they had but looked a bit light on paper. Some candidates just don't show that well...or interview that well.

I sat down with the hiring manager and started to tell the story of one of my most successful Placements. I didn't just rattle off the candidate's qualifications and experience—I painted a picture of who they were as a person. I talked about their passion for their work, their dedication to their craft, and the unique perspective they brought to the table.

As I spoke, I could see the client's eyes light up. They started to lean in, hanging on every word. I then pivoted to the candidate they were considering. Were they looking for a professional resume writer or master interviewer? No, they wanted someone who could visually translate their ideas to the marketplace. And by the time I finished, they were sold. They understood, on a visceral level, the value that this candidate could bring to their organization.

Since then, I've made storytelling a core part of my business. Every time I present a candidate to a client, I don't just focus on their resume—I focus on their story. I talk about their journey, their challenges, and their triumphs. I help the client see them not just as a set of skills and experience, but as a living, breathing human being with a unique perspective and a valuable contribution to make.

And you know what? It works. Time and time again, I've seen the power of storytelling in action. It's helped me win over skeptical clients, differentiate myself from competitors, and build lasting relationships with candidates and companies alike.

Of course, crafting a compelling story isn't always easy. It takes practice, patience, and a deep understanding of your audience. You have to know what resonates with them, what captures their attention, and what inspires them to take action.

But when you get it right, there's nothing quite like it. A well-crafted story can transform a simple business transaction into a meaningful, impactful experience. It can create a sense of connection, build trust, and inspire loyalty in ways that facts and figures alone simply can't.

43 MARKETING WATERFALLS

LET'S DIVE IN AND DISCOVER HOW TOP-PERFORMING RECRUITERS keep their pipelines full and their phones ringing.

I remember early in my recruiting career I was always curious about what set the Big Billers apart from the rest of us. What was their secret sauce? After years of studying their habits and strategies, I discovered a few key things:

1. They prioritize activity over everything else. While most recruiters are content to make a few calls here and there, the top dogs are dialing for dollars all day, every day.

2. They don't just work harder, they work smarter. Every call is carefully crafted, every voicemail is methodically scripted, every email is surgically precise.

3. They ooze confidence. Even in the face of rejection (and trust me, there's plenty of that in this business), they maintain an unshakeable belief in their ability to get the job done.

But the fourth thing was the real kicker. The true secret weapon of the heavy hitters is…drumroll please…MARKETING. That's right, the best of the best never stop promoting themselves and their services.

They understand that in order to score the juiciest job orders, they need to be front-of-mind with their clients at all times. But here's the thing: not all marketing is created equal. The 'spray and pray' approach of blasting out generic emails and making half-hearted cold calls just doesn't cut it anymore. To really dominate your niche, you need a more targeted, more strategic approach. Enter the 'Marketing Waterfall.' Think of it like a military operation. Before you deploy your troops, you need to 'shape the battlefield.' That means defining your target market and mapping out your plan of attack.

Start by carving out a specialty niche that you can realistically cover on a quarterly basis. The magic number seems to be around 1500 contacts, give or take. That might sound like a lot, but when you break it down, it's really only 25 calls per day. Totally doable, right?

Here's where the '4% rule' comes into play. Conventional wisdom says that you'll place with about 4% of the clients in your niche. So, if you've got 1500 contacts and you make 60 Placements a year at an average fee of $20K, boom—you're at $1.2 million. Not too shabby.

But not all clients are created equal. The real money is in what I call the '4% companies.' These are the clients that have an urgent need, a hard-to-fill role, or a proactive talent strategy. They're the ones that are willing to pay top dollar for top talent.

How do you find these unicorns? It all comes down to your marketing mix. The foundation of your outreach should be good old-fashioned phone calls. I know, I know—in the age of texting and tweeting, talking on the phone can feel a little old school. But trust me, there's no substitute for the power of the human voice.

When you do get a hiring manager on the line, don't just wing it. Come prepared with a compelling 'Most Placeable Candidate' presentation that showcases your recruiter chops. Use the 'Feature, Accomplishment, Benefit' format to really drive home your value prop.

But don't stop there. In between your phone blitzes, you should be peppering your niche with a steady stream of value-added content. Think market intel, salary data, industry trends—the kind of stuff that positions you as a true expert in your space.

You should also be leveraging the power of social proof through 'four-sends.' These are glowing testimonials from your satisfied clients and placed candidates that you can sprinkle throughout your outreach. Nothing builds credibility like a ringing endorsement from a happy customer.

That's the 'Marketing Waterfall' in action. Define your niche, identify your 4% companies, and unleash a torrent of high-value, high-touch, multi-channel marketing. It's not easy, but it's the surest path to recruiting domination.

I'll leave you with this quote from legendary ad man David Ogilvy, "You cannot bore people into buying your product. You can only interest them in buying it." Now, get out there and make some noise, fellow recruiters! Your next big Placement is just a phone call (or email, or LinkedIn message) away.

44 BEST YEAR EVER

LET'S DIVE INTO THE WORLD OF HABIT FORMATION AND discover how small, incremental improvements can lead to remarkable results over time. James Clear, in his book "Atomic Habits," argues that real change comes from the compound effect of hundreds of small decisions and habits—what he calls 'atomic habits.' The idea is that if you can just get 1% better each day, you'll end up with results that are 37 times better after a year.

But how can we apply this concept to recruiting and goal setting? It all starts with what I call the 'Five Central Principles of Goal Setting':

1. Write your goals down. If they're not on paper, they're just wishes.
2. Vividly imagine the outcome. Create a mental movie of what success looks like.
3. Deeply desire the goal. You've got to want it and want it badly.

4. Fully commit to the process. No half-measures or hedging your bets.
5. Get an accountability partner. Someone to keep you honest and on track.

With these principles in mind, it's time to focus on developing the habits that will make success inevitable. The key is to make your good habits obvious, attractive, easy, and satisfying. For example, you can make your daily planner front-and-center on your desk, so you can't miss it (obvious). Give yourself a little reward, like checking social media, after hitting your call goal for the day (attractive). Set up templates and scripts, so your calls and emails practically write themselves (easy). And keep a tally of your wins, like Placements and Send Outs, and celebrate each one (satisfying).

On the flip side, you want to make your bad habits invisible, unattractive, hard, and unsatisfying. That might mean deleting time-wasting apps and blocking distracting websites on your work computer (invisible), making a pact with your accountability partner to pay $20 for every day you miss your 100 point goal (unattractive), keeping your phone in another room while you're sourcing and recruiting (hard), and reflecting on how crappy you feel after a day of slacking off and letting yourself down (unsatisfying).

One of my favorite tools for tracking daily activities and ensuring progress towards goals is the previously mentioned Daily 100 Point Sheet. Each day, you'll track your activities and assign them a point value based on how directly they contribute to making a Placement. The goal is to hit at least 100 points per day. Trust me, it works.

The beauty of this approach is that it's not about overhauling your entire life overnight—it's about making small, incremental improvements that compound over time. And as you start to see results, you'll build momentum and confidence, which will fuel even more progress.

And that's my challenge to you: set some big, hairy, audacious goals for the year ahead. Break them down into quarterly targets and daily habits. And then, focus on getting just 1% better each day. If you can do that, I guarantee you'll be blown away by what you can achieve.

As the great Zig Ziglar once said, "You don't have to be great to start, but you have to start to be great." So, what are you waiting for? Let's make this your best year yet! Remember, success is not about perfection; it's about consistency. Focus on your atomic habits, and the results will take care of themselves.

45 DEAD HORSES

Let me tell you a story about a recruiter I once knew. We'll call him Jack. Jack was a hard worker, but he had a bad habit of hanging onto dead-end Job Orders and problem candidates way too long. He'd pour hours into searches that were going nowhere, chasing after hiring managers who had gone radio silent and candidates who were clearly just using him for leverage.

One day, Jack's manager pulled him aside and handed him a copy of Seth Godin's book "The Dip." The manager said, "Jack, you've got to learn when to quit. Not everything is worth your time and effort. Focus on the opportunities with the best ROI." Jack was skeptical, but he gave the book a read. And it was a revelation.

Godin argues that winners win because they know when to quit. They understand the concept of opportunity cost—that every hour spent on a low-probability deal is an hour not spent on a high-probability one. He introduces the idea of 'the dip'—the long slog between starting and mastering something. The dip is where most people give up. But those who push through to the other side reap massive rewards because scarcity creates value.

The key is knowing the difference between a dip and a cul-de-sac. A dip is temporary—you'll get through it if you persist. But a cul-de-sac will never get better, no matter how hard you try. The superstars are the ones who can tell the difference and have the guts to quit the cul-de-sacs. This really hit home for Jack. He realized he'd been wasting time on way too many cul-de-sacs—the 'always looking' hiring managers, the candidates who wouldn't return calls, the Purple Squirrel job orders. Meanwhile, he was neglecting the dips—the winnable deals that required persistence and problem-solving.

So, Jack made a change. He got ruthless about qualifying his Job Orders and candidates upfront. He set clear milestones and drop-dead dates. And if things weren't progressing, he cut bait and moved on—no guilt, no excuses.

The results were dramatic. Jack's Send Outs and Placements skyrocketed. He was working smarter, not just harder. And he had a lot more time and mental energy to invest in business development and candidate generation. But Jack didn't just get better at quitting. He also got savvier about what to pursue in the first place. He took a hard look at his niche and realized he was spreading himself too thin.

He narrowed his focus to a specific industry and function where he could really stand out. He set a goal to become the undisputed 'best in the world' in his space. And he put all his resources into dominating that market— building relationships, establishing thought leadership, delivering unparalleled service.

Within a year, Jack was the top biller in his office. And it all started with learning when to say "No" so he could go all-in on the right "Yeses." Because here's the thing: being the best in your niche has exponential benefits. The rewards are massively skewed to the top performers. It's not uncommon for the #1 player to out bill the #10 player by 10X or more. That's the power of what Godin calls the 'Zipf's Law' distribution.

But you'll never get there if you're bogged down servicing duds and chasing fool's errands. You have to protect your time and attention like the precious resources they are and deploy them where they'll yield the highest return.

The moral of Jack's story is this: get great at quitting. Have the discipline to walk away from the wrong opportunities so you can double down on the right ones. Narrow your focus and strive to be the dominant force in your market. Do that, and you won't just survive in this business—you'll thrive beyond your wildest expectations. The dead horses will fade in your rearview as you gallop towards greener pastures. And that, my friends, is a beautiful thing.

WHEN OBSTACLES ARE THROWN in your way, you need to evaluate the new situation and change your behavior accordingly. Unfortunately, it is a fact of life that when a human being learns a task, and new circumstances present themselves so that alternative measures are indicated, the human being will take the path of least resistance and revert back to the task they have learned, even if it doesn't work, as opposed to learning a new task to handle the new situation.

To better understand this principle, let me tell you a story from back in April 1945 near the end of WWII.

WWII in the Pacific was approaching its stormy conclusion. It was April 1945 off Okinawa. Three Japanese kamikazes dove out of low cloud cover attacking the American destroyer, USS Hazelwood (DD531). The ship maneuvered to avoid two of the planes, but the third came in low and from astern. This plane was hit by Hazelwood's anti-aircraft fire, careened past the superstructure, and hit the port side, smashing into the bridge and exploding. It was a devastating suicide attack. In the aftermath, it was determined that the ship had no bridge, no gun mounts, no torpedo tubes, and many human casualties. Ten officers and 67 enlisted men were killed, including the Commanding Officer. To put it bluntly, the Hazelwood needed help.

As luck would have it, Hazelwood's sister ship, the destroyer USS Trathen (DD530) was nearby. From the Trathen, the best helmsman and navigator was transferred to the Hazelwood. That man was John Schuhmacher, known as 'Chief Shoe.' He was Trathen's 20-year veteran and a Pearl Harbor survivor, a master navigator who would be assigned, with minimal tools and help, the unprecedented task of navigating the badly damaged ship and diminished crew, first to the nearby island of Ulithi, then on to Pearl Harbor, and finally back to San Diego for repairs.

Under normal conditions, navigating a ship at sea in those days before computers and satellite position locators was a laborious and painstaking process. But with the Hazelwood, the bridge didn't exist anymore, and all of the officers who could help were dead. Chief Shoe was forced to navigate from a temporary command location by magnetic compass and emergency 'after steering.' And all of this in enemy waters. This was a new circumstance and so very rarely attempted. But Chief Shoe, with minimal navigational aids, successfully brought the Hazelwood back to safety. He readily adapted to this new and severe situation into which he was thrown.

Adaptation in any business is often explained by understanding 'The Principle of Requisite Variety.' The textbook definition of this principle is that, in any 'closed-loop' system—electronics or human communications, for example—the element with the most variables always controls the outcome. What this means in layman's terms is that you need to be 'noted for your flexibility.'

Historically, superstars and Big Billers have learned to adapt when confronted with new and unique circumstances and have learned to be flexible and change when necessary.

Years after the Hazelwood disaster, I spoke to Chief Shoe (then a Warrant Officer) about those days on the crippled Hazelwood and how he adapted. He said he had no choice. He had to be flexible in order to carry out his mission and save his sister ship and its crew. He said that it was a lesson that many of his shipmates were forced to learn during the ravages of the war they were fighting. He and his shipmates became masters of flexibility when the situation called for it. This was indeed The Greatest Generation!

Full Disclosure: I had a special relationship with Chief Shoe. You see, to me, John was merely known as Grandpa Schuhmacher.

46 MAKE IT SCALABLE

THERE IS A DIRTY SECRET IN THE RECRUITING INDUSTRY THAT few people talk about. Growing your business is difficult, attempting to do it alone can feel impossible. As a rainmaker or solo producer, there is a finite limit to the amount of Job Orders you can work and candidates you can place.

Now, you, like many of us, may make a very good income from that solo effort, but is it sustainable? Can you afford to take a decent vacation? What happens to your business if you are sick or injured?

The term that seems to be sticking these days is 'Scalable,' which simply means replicating the success you are having at higher levels. Before you start this you really need to be laser focused on your 'growth mindset.' That means you have fine-tuned your business model, systematized both your marketing approach as well as your candidate pipeline, and established your fees in your specialty niche(s). If we are borrowing from the more trendy lexicon, we call this optimization.

In essence, you are developing a system of success. It is repeatable, predictable, and profitable. Now, there are three basic ways to scale your recruiting business.

1. Work harder - not that much fun, leads to mistakes, and kills the passion. Also, most of us like to sleep at least a few hours each night. Still, this is the one I see most of us leaning into as we try to scale from where we are to that magical land of Big Billers.

2. Using Technology - and I am talking all tech, from the contact database you prize to that pricey LinkedIn Recruiter account. Maybe you are using AI systems to fill in the gaps or speed up your client touches. An email Drip campaign that automates your 'personal' emails. Am I against tech? Not at all, many times it is exactly what your firm needs to be doing to make Placements. The lure of tech is that it is a magical fix, and we start believing in it more than the process.

3. Increase your Recruiters - this is my personal preference mainly because this is a people business. That means that your systems need to be bullet-proof, and you need to put in as much care selecting a new recruiter as you would a candidate for your best client, and you need to provide exceptional training and ongoing coaching.

If your desk is a manufacturing plant, then your next goal is to build an industrial park full of recruiting desks operating at peak efficiency just like you. But what if, you say, "I'm working in a small subset of FinTech, and I don't think the space has capacity for more recruiters."

If you were my coaching client, I would likely suggest you reexamine your niche; you may have specialized too narrowly. It's good to be the 'go-to' guy or gal in your specialty, but if it's that small, you are going to have a hard time growing, even by yourself. You also risk financial collapse if a negative disruption impacts that niche. Step back to the next larger level and see if the same processes and connections don't work there as well.

Back to scaling, though. The thing is, you don't necessarily have to add more recruiters in your specialty or even in your one location. The modern remote offices function just as well from thousands of miles away and work from home recruiters can save you tons of overhead. My personal suggestion is to add recruiting desks strategically in related fields instead of wildly divergent specialties (although these can work as well). If you don't understand the niche your recruiter is working, though, you may struggle to properly train or manage them.

I'll add one more thing here. It may be that you don't need to add recruiters to scale to the next level. Where are you spending your time each workday? You may find that what you really need is an administrative assistant or a talent sourcer to locate new candidates. Adding that specialty help can free you up to focus on making more marketing calls and completing more Placements. You can advertise for help on numerous sites, and if you are okay with off-shore help, you may find it costing you much less than you expected.

47 ATTAINING MASTERY

As I reflect on my journey in the recruiting industry, I realize that the true art of closing a deal extends far beyond the initial Placement. It's a multi-step process that requires diligence, foresight, and a genuine commitment to building lasting relationships with clients.

The first Placement, the service sell, is just the beginning. It's the moment when you successfully match a candidate with a client's needs and agreement is made, and it's a cause for celebration. However, the real work begins after this point. Two to four days after start date, I make it a point to follow up with the client, conducting a thorough consultation to ensure that the Placement is meeting their expectations. This follow-up serves two crucial purposes: it demonstrates my dedication to their success, and it allows me to uncover additional problem openings that need to be addressed.

We often already know of one other opening. The candidate we placed has left a vacancy in their previous role, presenting yet another opportunity for me to fill that position as well. By proactively identifying and addressing these needs, I can effectively cover the cost of acquiring a new customer, making the initial service revenue pure profit.

Fast forward to Day 30, and I'm ready for the third point of sale. At this point, I've received the full fee, and any guarantees in the contract have likely been fulfilled. This is the perfect time to reach out and request testimonials, reviews, and referrals from the satisfied client. It's incredible how many new orders I generate simply by following up one more time. It's a testament to the fact that my recruiting desk is a well-oiled manufacturing plant, where no single phase stops just because I've successfully delivered a product to a new customer.

In the world of recruiting, where the landscape is constantly shifting, it's crucial to stay ahead of the curve. As James Clear said, "It is not too late to do what you want to do—if you stop waiting for the time to be right."

This mindset has been a driving force behind my success, pushing me to embrace new challenges and opportunities with enthusiasm and determination.

One of the most valuable lessons I've learned is the importance of building genuine relationships. As Dr. Ivan Misner, the founder of BNI, emphasizes, "Networking is not about hunting. It is about farming. It's about cultivating relationships." By focusing on nurturing connections with clients, candidates, and colleagues, I've been able to create a robust network that has been instrumental in my growth as a recruiter.

Another key aspect of mastery is the willingness to learn from others who have paved the way. Just as Robocruiter and the others I have profiled in these pages, I've been fortunate to have incredible mentors in the recruiting space who have generously shared their knowledge and experience with me. By studying their techniques, adopting their best practices, and adapting them to my own style, I've been able to accelerate my progress, achieve remarkable results and share these big biller techniques with those I train and coach.

Ultimately, becoming a master in the recruiting business requires a combination of hard work, dedication, and a growth mindset. In a growth mindset, people believe that their most basic abilities can be developed through dedication and hard work—brains and talent are just the starting point. By embracing this philosophy and consistently pushing myself to learn, improve, and innovate, I know that I can continue to thrive in this dynamic and rewarding industry.

"The future is not some place we are going to, but one we are creating. The paths are not to be found but made. And the activity of making them changes both the maker and the destination."

- JOHN SCHARR

---

48 LIES THAT DOOM US

You know, its funny, we recruiters are a passionate bunch. We pour our hearts and souls into this business, honing our craft, sharpening our skills, always striving to be the best. And yet, for all that dedication and drive, extraordinary results can still feel maddeningly out of reach.

So, what gives? Why do we sometimes fall short of the success we're chasing, even when we've got the passion and the chops to make it happen?

According to Gary Keller in his book "The One Thing," there are six sneaky little lies that can derail us on the path to greatness. Let's break them down:

Lie #1: Everything matters equally. In the immortal words of Dwight Schrute, "False."

The truth is, in the real world, things are never equal. Some activities and priorities will always yield a higher return than others. The key is to identify and focus relentlessly on the vital few, not the trivial many.

This is where tools like the 80/20 Principle come in handy. Also known as the 'Pareto Principle,' it states that a minority of causes (roughly 20%) are responsible for a majority of effects (roughly 80%).

In recruiting, this might mean that a small handful of clients generate the bulk of your billings, or that a few key activities (like marketing and recruiting) drive most of your results. The lesson? Don't get bogged down in the small stuff.

Ruthlessly prioritize the people and practices that move the needle and let the rest fade into the background.

Lie #2: Multitasking is the key to productivity.

Oh, if only this were true! The siren song of multitasking is strong, especially in the age of constant pings and dings and notifications. But study after study has shown that humans are terrible at task-switching. It's not multitasking—it's just rapid toggling between activities, and it comes with a heavy cognitive cost.

Every time you bounce between tasks, you lose time and focus as your brain reorients to the new context.

Mistakes become more likely, stress levels rise, and true engagement suffers. The smarter play is to go all-in on one thing at a time, giving it your full and undivided attention before moving on to the next. Single tasking for the win!

Lie #3: Discipline is the answer.

Ah, discipline. That elusive, slippery quality we all wish we had more of. But here's the thing: willpower is a finite resource. Relying on it alone to muscle through challenges is a recipe for burnout and frustration.

The wiser approach is to build habits and systems that automate good behaviors and make success all but inevitable. As the saying goes, "Motivation gets you started, but habit keeps you going."

Focus on cultivating the right routines, and discipline becomes almost effortless.

Lie #4: Willpower is always on call. Speaking of willpower, it's not a 24/7 resource. Studies show that our reserves of self-control are highest in the morning and gradually deplete throughout the day as we make more and more choices.

That's why it's so important to tackle your most important work early, when your willpower is fresh, and your energy is high. Save the low-stakes busywork for later in the day when your brain is running on fumes. By matching your tasks to your willpower levels, you'll get more done with less struggle.

Lie #5: A balanced life is ideal.

This one is tough, because work-life balance is held up as the holy grail of modern existence. But the reality is, extraordinary results often require extraordinary focus and commitment. You can't expect to reach the pinnacle of your field by giving it the same time and attention as everything else.

The key is to reframe the question from "How can I achieve balance?" to "What should I prioritize right now?" Sometimes that means going all-in on work for a season. Other times, it means stepping back to focus on family, health, or personal growth.

The goal is not constant equilibrium, but intentional counterbalancing based on your values and goals.

Lie #6: Big is bad.

In a world of 'lean' this and 'minimum viable' that, it's easy to get sucked into a scarcity mindset. But playing small serves no one, least of all yourself. Dreaming big, setting audacious goals, and reaching for the stars is what separates the good from the truly great.

Will you fail sometimes? Absolutely. But failure is just part of the journey. The real risk lies not in aiming too high and missing the mark, but in aiming too low and hitting it. So, dare to go big and bold. You might just surprise yourself with what you're capable of.

At the end of the day, those are the six pernicious lies that can hold us back from our true potential.

By calling them out and consciously counteracting them, we can clear the path for the extraordinary results we crave. It all comes down to focus. "Cutting through the noise and honing in on the 'one thing' that will make everything else easier or unnecessary," as Keller puts it.

When you bring that kind of clarity and single-minded commitment to your recruiting practice, incredible things start to happen.

Deals that once seemed out of reach suddenly become doable. Candidates who once played hard to get are suddenly eager to take your call. And clients who once viewed you as just another vendor are now treating you like a trusted partner.

That's the power of identifying and pursuing your 'one thing' with everything you've got. Take a hard look at your desk, your business, your life. What's the single most important activity or priority that will move the needle for you? Once you've got it, go after it with all the passion and discipline you can muster.

Because that, my friends, is how the extraordinary becomes your new ordinary. And trust me—it's a pretty extraordinary feeling.

Part 7 | The Future

"Success is not about where you are today, but where you'll be tomorrow."
- UNKNOWN

49 MOTIVATION

Lou Scott was not only a master of recruitment techniques, but also a firm believer in the power of motivation. He understood that success in any field, including recruiting, hinges on an individual's desire and drive to achieve their goals. Lou often shared stories that illustrated this point, captivating his audience and leaving a lasting impact on their hearts and minds.

One such story, borrowed from coach Bobby Bowden's autobiography, tells the tale of a young defensive tackle at Georgetown University in the 1920s. Despite his unwavering dedication and hard work, the player struggled to improve his performance on the field. However, tragedy struck just days before his final game when his father passed away.

The young man pleaded with his coach, Lou Little, to start him in the championship game, hoping to honor his father's memory. Although hesitant at first, Little was moved by the player's determination and granted his wish. What followed was a remarkable display of passion and skill, as the young man played the game of his life, leading his team to victory and a conference championship.

After the game, when asked what had sparked such an incredible performance, the player revealed that his father had been blind, and this was the first time he could see his son play. This poignant revelation underscores the immense power of motivation and the depths of human potential when fueled by a strong sense of purpose.

Lou Scott's use of this story serves as a reminder that success is not solely dependent on technique or skill, but rather on the burning desire within each individual to achieve their goals. He encouraged his audience not to wait for a life-altering event to spur them into action, but to seize the moment and pursue their dreams with unwavering dedication.

In the world of recruiting, this message is particularly resonant. Building relationships, identifying top talent, and closing deals all require a level of persistence and passion that cannot be taught through training alone. It is the recruiter's own motivation and drive that will ultimately determine their success in this competitive and dynamic field.

As we reflect on Lou Scott's wisdom and the stories he shared, we are reminded of the importance of cultivating a strong sense of purpose and motivation in our personal and professional lives. By tapping into our own yearning to succeed and making a positive impact, we can overcome obstacles, inspire others, and achieve greatness in the face of adversity.

50 THE DIRECT TECHNIQUE

The Big Biller (BB) Direct Recruiting Technique

THE INITIAL CALL:

About 60 seconds in length. Our BB says:

> "I would like to call you sometime this week — some evening — what time would be best? I would like to discuss some alternative job opportunities with you, and I'll need about 30 minutes."

Big Biller refuses to talk to the potential recruit on this initial call.

BB wants the potential recruit thinking about talking to a recruiter.

You don't need a JO (Job Order) to do this.

Never miss the call back time—it illustrates your punctuality.

The Second Call:

The BB asks first,

> "If you were to make a change, what position would that be for?"

The BB then asks,

> "What are your geographical limitations?"

Don't talk specifics—take a Recruit Data Sheet (RDS)—explain the FAB.

At the end of the call the BB will say,

> "I don't know enough about you now. I'll review all of my searches, and if there are any matches, I'll call you back. I do promise, at this stage, not to mention your name or your company's name."

Then hang up.

The key to this is developing relationships—establishing rapport.

The Third Call:

Now is the time to present a position. If the recruit doesn't have the right parameters, our BB tells them,

> "My companies won't consider people without _____."

If the recruit does match, this is when BB arranges the first client-candidate meeting.

Be Persistent

Regardless of your recruiting effort results, always call back after 2-3 days with a new piece of information and a condensed re-presentation of your FAB'ed JO. You need to give these folks time to think about what you have asked them. Lead suggestions will come to them with time, but don't expect them to initiate the call to you with this information. You must call them back. You must ask again. When you do this, don't be surprised if your hit rate improves dramatically.

Challenge Yourself to be the Best You Can Be

I would like to quote again President John Kennedy who spoke one September day in 1962 about why we were accepting the challenge of going to the moon. This is what he said:

"We choose to go to the moon. We choose to go to the moon in this decade and do the other things, not because they are easy, but because they are hard, because that goal will serve to organize and measure the best of our energies and skills, because that challenge is one that we are willing to accept, one we are unwilling to postpone, and one which we intend to win, and the others, too."

I, too, have a challenge. I want to challenge you recruiters, you salespeople and you entrepreneurs to do the parts of your individual businesses correctly—not because it's easy, but because it's hard. And because, as President Kennedy promised, the attainment of our goals will serve to organize and measure the best of our energies and skills. And, at the end of the day, this is how we can evaluate ourselves on the scales of success.

51 SIGNALS AND NOISE

BACK IN MY DAYS IN NAVY INTELLIGENCE WE HAD AN ONGOING mission to monitor radio traffic in the Mediterranean and separate what were verifiable radio traffic or 'Signals' from the background 'Noise.' The challenge: many times they are nearly indistinguishable. However, one may be of vital importance while the other is simply distracting. In our daily business life how do we separate the two?

In my coaching, I teach that there are six essential activities that separate the high-earning recruiters from the pack.

First up, a quick story. Early in my career, I had the chance to shadow one of the top billers in our firm for a day. I'll never forget the laser-like focus this guy had from the moment he walked in the door.

No chitchat, no coffee breaks, no scrolling through ESPN.com. He was a machine.

The first thing he did was review his hot sheet—the Send-Outs and interviews he had lined up for the day. He knew that nothing else mattered if he didn't have butts in seats. Then he fired up his CRM and started dialing for dollars. MPC presentations, recruiting calls, client check-ins—he was a maestro on the phone.

What struck me most was how he handled the inevitable objections and brush-offs. Where most recruiters would get flustered or frustrated, he had an almost zen-like calm. He knew that every "No" just got him closer to a "Yes." It was like watching a master class in resilience and persistence. By lunchtime, he had already booked three new Send Outs and taken a Job Order. I was in awe. When I asked him his secret, he just smiled and said, "Kid, if it don't make dollars, it don't make sense. Focus on the money-making activities and tune out the rest."

That advice has stuck with me to this day, and it's the core of what separates the top earners from the rest of the pack. Let's break it down:

1. Focus on the activities that lead directly to Placements. Send Outs, interviews, offers, closes. Everything else is just noise.

2. Embrace the phone as your moneymaker. The more conversations you have, the more relationships you build, the more opportunities you uncover. Period.

3. Hone your presentation until it sizzles. Whether you're selling a candidate or selling your services, your ability to articulate value is everything.

4. Work every desk in your niche, every day. The law of averages is on your side—the more lines you have in the water, the more fish you'll reel in.

5. Be picky about the openings you work. Not all Job Orders are created equal, and your time is your most precious asset. Stick to the 20% that will generate 80% of your Placements.

6. Track your metrics religiously. What gets measured gets improved.

Use a tool such as the 100-point sheet to keep yourself honest and on track.

Now, a quick detour to talk about the importance of focus in today's distraction-filled world. We live in an age of constant pings, dings, and rings—it's no wonder our attention spans are shot. But as a recruiter, your ability to zero in on the task at hand is absolutely critical.

That means setting clear boundaries around your time and attention. It means being ruthless about prioritization. And it means training your brain to resist the siren song of shiny objects and stick to the plan.

One technique that I've found incredibly helpful is time-blocking. Carve out dedicated chunks of time for your most important activities—sourcing, recruiting, marketing, etc.—and treat them as sacred. No email, no social media, no watercooler chatter. Just you and the work.

It's not easy, especially in the beginning. But like any muscle, your focus will strengthen with practice. And the payoff in productivity and performance is huge.

Always keep in mind— the six core activities that will make you rich (or at least richer) as a recruiter. But here's the thing: knowing isn't doing. It's up to you to take these principles and put them into action, every single day.

It won't always be easy. There will be days when the phone feels heavy, and the rejections sting. There will be times when the distractions seem overwhelming, and the momentum feels gone. But that's when you dig deep, remember your 'why', and keep pushing forward.

Because at the end of the day, this business is a numbers game. And the recruiters who win are the ones who show up, day after day, and do the work. They're the ones who trust the process, even when the results aren't immediate. And they're the ones who never, ever quit.

Here's my challenge to you: pick one of these six activities and commit to mastering it over the next week. Whether it's making more marketing calls, crafting a killer MPC presentation, or tracking your metrics more diligently, pour your heart and soul into it. Then watch as the momentum starts to build, and the Placements start to flow.

Remember, success in this business is not an accident. It's the predictable result of consistent, focused, high-value action. Get out there and make it happen. And always, always keep your eye on the prize: "If it don't make dollars, it don't make sense."

52 A PROVEN METHOD

Lou Scott was a visionary in the world of recruiting, and his impact on the industry is still felt today. As one of the driving forces behind Management Recruiters International (MRI), Lou developed and refined many of the recruitment techniques that have become standard practice in the field.

One of Lou's most enduring contributions was the concept of the Most Placeable Candidate, or MPC, which we discussed in Chapter Seven. This approach revolutionized the way recruiters marketed their candidates to potential employers. Lou taught us that an MPC should possess five key qualities: a marketable skill, a realistic outlook, the ability to interview and start within a reasonable timeframe, strong references, and a respectful attitude toward the recruiter as a professional.

Beyond these core qualities, Lou also emphasized the importance of targeting candidates who were currently employed, held mid-level positions, and were willing to commit to daily communication and exclusivity with their recruiter during the job search process.

To ensure that a candidate truly met the MPC criteria, Lou developed a set of qualifying questions that delved into the candidate's motivations, job search history, and overall commitment to making a career move. These questions served as a way to gauge the candidate's seriousness and to anticipate any potential obstacles down the line.

While some in the industry have criticized the MPC approach as being too focused on making a Placement rather than understanding the client's needs, Lou understood that the MPC was simply a vehicle for opening doors and building rapport with hiring managers. By presenting a high-caliber candidate right off the bat, recruiters could demonstrate their value and start a conversation that might lead to other job orders or opportunities.

Ultimately, Lou's MPC strategy was about more than just making a single Placement. It was about establishing trust, credibility, and long-term relationships with both candidates and clients. Lou believed that by consistently delivering top talent and exceptional service, recruiters could become indispensable partners to their clients, earning the right to be kept in the loop on all of their hiring needs.

For Lou, recruiting was more than just a job—it was a calling. He had a deep love for the industry and a genuine desire to help others succeed. His legacy lives on through the countless recruiters who have adopted his techniques and philosophies, and who continue to shape the future of the field.

As we navigate the challenges and opportunities of the modern recruitment landscape, we would do well to remember the lessons of giants like Lou. By focusing on the fundamentals, prioritizing relationships, and always striving to deliver the best possible candidates and service, we can build thriving careers and make a lasting impact on the lives of those we serve.

53 WHAT COMES NEXT

THE GLOBAL PANDEMIC OF 2020 UPENDED LIFE AS WE KNEW IT, leaving a trail of shuttered businesses and shattered routines in its wake.

The recruiting landscape is hardly recognizable, and you're wondering if you've stumbled into some dystopian alternate reality. Welcome to the world of the post-apocalyptic recruiter.

But fear not, my friends. While the pandemic is in our rearview mirror, many of the challenges it caused are real, and the changes are profound. That being said, I maintain that the core principles of great recruiting remain as true as ever. In fact, I'd argue that mastering the fundamentals is more important now than it's ever been.

Let's talk about what's changed, what hasn't, and how to not just survive, but thrive in this brave new world.

First, the obvious: Remote work is here to stay. The genie is out of the bottle, and there's no putting it back. According to a recent study by McKinsey, 20-25% of the workforce could work from home 3-5 days a week without any loss in productivity.

That's a seismic shift that has implications for everything from talent pools to office leases.

As recruiters, we need to be on the front lines of this conversation, advising our clients on the risks and rewards of various workplace models. The spectrum runs from fully remote to fully in-person, with a whole lot of hybrid arrangements in between. Each option comes with its own set of tradeoffs, and it's our job to help hiring managers navigate those choices. But here's the thing: While the logistics may have changed, the underlying psychology of career decisions remains largely the same. Candidates still crave challenge, growth, and purpose.

They still want to work for companies that align with their values and invest in their development. And they still respond to recruiters who take the time to understand their unique goals and motivations. In other words, the human element of recruiting is more important than ever. In a world of Zoom interviews and virtual onboarding, the personal touch is what sets great recruiters apart.

How do we cultivate that human connection in the age of social distancing? It starts with mastering the basics: building rapport, asking great questions, and listening more than we talk. It means being a trusted advisor, not just a transactional order-taker. And it requires a relentless focus on the candidate experience, from first outreach to final offer.

But beyond the soft skills, there are some hard truths we need to confront as well. Chief among them is the sobering reality of candidate ghosting. Even before the pandemic, no-shows and radio silence were on the rise. In a remote-first world, the problem has only gotten worse.

The solution? A return to rigorous qualifying, both on the client and candidate sides. We can't afford to waste time on Job Orders that aren't real, or on candidates who aren't serious. We need to dig deeper in our intake calls, asking tough questions and setting clear expectations. And we need to stay in consistent communication with our candidates, reinforcing the opportunity and our commitment at every step.

Which brings me to another crucial point: In a market where top talent gets snapped up in days (if not hours), we can't afford to let perfect be the enemy of good. We need to move fast, while still being thorough.

That means streamlining our processes, leveraging technology, and making decisions quickly. It also means setting tight timelines with our clients and holding them accountable to interview promptly and provide timely feedback.

At the same time, we can't sacrifice quality for quantity. The best recruiters are always looking to level up their game, whether that's honing their presentation, expanding their network, or deepening their market expertise. In a world of constant change, ongoing learning is non-negotiable.

Where does that leave us? With a daunting but exhilarating challenge. As post-apocalyptic recruiters, we have the opportunity to shape the future of work in real time. We get to be strategic partners, culture champions, and talent oracles, all rolled into one.

But to do that, we need to double down on what's always mattered most: relationships, curiosity, and grit. We need to be students of human behavior and masters of our craft. And above all, we need to remember that even in the darkest of times, great recruiters are a beacon of hope and possibility.

So, strap on your proverbial armor and sharpen your metaphorical swords. The war for talent rages on, and the world needs heroes like you on the front lines. It won't be easy, but nothing worthwhile ever is. And who knows? You just might find that the post-apocalyptic landscape suits you. After all, when the old rules no longer apply, the only limit is your own imagination. Dream big, fight hard, and never stop believing in the power of human potential. The future is yours to recruit.

I wish you all great success in your recruitment business, and I hope we get to meet at some point. But for now, I have to go. My phone is ringing...

I wish you the best!

REM

ABOUT THE AUTHOR

Bob Marshall is a renowned business expert with over 44 years of experience in the recruiting professional services industry. Throughout his career, he has held various leadership roles, including Manager, VP, President, Coach, and Trainer. This diverse background has equipped him with a unique understanding of the challenges and opportunities faced by businesses and professionals across different sectors.

Bob's impressive achievements have been recognized with numerous awards, including the Million Dollar Hall of Fame Award, and he has been acknowledged as a top trainer in his field. His success is a testament to his dedication, expertise, and commitment to helping professionals and businesses thrive.

As the founder of The Elite Recruiter Masterclass and The Marshall Plan, Bob has empowered countless professionals worldwide, providing them with the tools, strategies, and guidance needed to excel in their careers. His comprehensive training programs have been delivered across the US, UK, Malta, and Cyprus, demonstrating the global reach and impact of his work.

Known for his integrity, generosity, and passion for sharing knowledge, Bob has made a significant impact on the business world. His expertise and guidance have inspired and motivated professionals across various industries, helping them to achieve their goals and drive success for their organizations.

Today, Bob continues to live and work on his horse ranch in McDonough, Georgia, where he remains dedicated to supporting and empowering professionals and businesses through his innovative training programs and services. His commitment to excellence and his ability to adapt to the ever-changing business landscape make him a valuable asset to any organization seeking to achieve growth and success.

Bob can be reached at bob@themarshallplan.org or at 770-898-5550. www.themarshallplan.org

7

www.ingramcontent.com/pod-product-compliance
Lightning Source LLC
LaVergne TN
LVHW091546070526
838199LV00023B/554/J